Business Communication

PUNEET GUPTA MBA
Assistant Professor
ICM and IEL, Dehradun, Uttarakhand

AN ISO 9001:2008 CERTIFIED COMPANY
Vayu Education of India
2/25, Ansari Road, Darya Ganj, New Delhi-110 002

Business Communication

ISBN: 978-93-80712-64-2

First Edition: 2010
Reprint: 2013

Price: ₹160.00

Printed & bound in India

Published by:
AN ISO 9001:2008 CERTIFIED COMPANY
VAYU EDUCATION OF INDIA
2/25, Ansari Road, Darya Ganj, New Delhi-110 002
Ph.: 91-11-47236600, 41564445
Fax: 91-11-41564440
E-mail: vei@veiindia.com
Web: www.veiindia.com

PREFACE

This book is basically designed for students who are eager to learn business communication; it addresses the practical and physical aspects of how to become agile and effective, by not spending any real effort on the why question, or on the question of what to do with it once you have better communication ability.

In view of widening gap between teacher and taught and spoiled educational environment, I have written this book in the best interest of the students. The book is presented in a simple, concise manner such that the reading is made pleasurable; the content and vocabulary encompasses on giving added meaning to the subject, it help students to understand current corporate strategic public relation and the subject in a better manner. It can, therefore, guide students in a proper direction and towards their ultimate and real goal of life.

"One is able to respond to proactive strategic direction, and being able to respond to reactive necessity, is what this book is about"

I hope that this book will be found useful to the teachers as well as students. Apart from it your suggestions are always welcome for improving the standards of the book.

I crave the indulgence of the readers for any printing mistakes in the book. I hope this book will serve the purpose of the student of various statuses, and only can judge how much I have succeeded in my efforts.

Puneet Gupta

ACKNOWLEDGEMENT

I gratefully acknowledge and express deep aspiration to many wonderful people who have given inspiration to furnish work with confidence.

I would like to give my special thanks and undying gratitude to all the people who gave us constructive inputs, positive support and there valuable contributions without which this book would not have reached its goals.

- To those through whose lives and writings has come the wisdom of the ages. We have tried to learn from your legacy.
- To our colleagues, clients and seminar participants whose deep sharing and synergy have moved us many levels beyond our own thinking.

Though it is difficult to thank everyone individually, it is my pleasure to express my gratitude to Dr. Rajiv Kumar Jain (Managing Director), Prof. Sanjeev Kumar Sharma (Chairperson) of Vayu Education of India, Darya Ganj, New Delhi. I would also like to thank Mr. Vijay Kumar Saini (Production Manager), Mr. Jitender Kumar Sharma (Sr. Sales Executive) and other production team members of Vayu Education of India, who published the book within a short duration in order to deliver a good quality book for the students who will really be benefited when they go through this book.

Finally, yet importantly, I would like to express my heartfelt thanks to my beloved parents for their blessings, my friends for their help and inspiration and motivation to present this book to you all.

Puneet Gupta

REVIEWING COMMITTEE

Name

Business Communication

According to Prescribed Syllabus
for
B.B.A. Ist First Semester
of
H.N.B. Garhwal University (Uttarakhand)

SYLLABUS

BBA Ist Semester
H.N.B. Garhwal University, Uttarakhand

103-Business Communication

Objective

The objective of the Course is to acquaint the students with the knowledge of the Communication written as well as oral required in the Corporate World in its day to day functioning.

COURSE CONTENTS

(*i*) **English Grammer:** Proper Uses of Verb, Noun, Adverb, Adjectives, Punctuation, Para Phrasing in Business Communication, Understanding Direct and Indirect Narration, Skills of Essay Writing and Precis Writing, Significance of knowledge of Grammer in Business Communication.

(*ii*) Basic Forms of Communication, Communication Models, Communication Process, Barriers and Bottlenecks in Communication, Corporate Communication: Formal and Informal Communication Networks, Grapevine, Non Verbal Communication. Importance of Communication in Business World.

(*iii*) **Letter Writing:** Principles, Structure, Planning, Drafting, Writing, Re-Writing, Editing, Different Types of Letters, Memos in Business Communications, Modern Office Techniques used in Business Communication.

(*iv*) Oral Communications, Public Speaking, Body Language, Presentations before the Group, Factors Affecting Presentation, Effective Listening, Interviewing Skills, Arranging and Participation in Group Discussion, Seminars and Conferences.

(*v*) **Report Writing:** Writing Skills, Planning, Drafting, Writing, Re-Writing, Editing, Different Types of Business reports, Structure, Steps Towards Writing of Different Types of Business reports, Style of Report Writings.

SUGGESTED READINGS

Gupta, Puneet	Business Communication
Sharma	Business Correspondence and Report Writing
Monipally	The Craft of Business Letter Writing
Lesikan V Raymond and Pettel E	Basic Business Communications
Herta and Murthy	Effective Business Communications

TABLE OF CONTENTS

CHAPTER-1

Basic of English Grammar

IMPORTANCE OF ENGLISH LANGUAGE

Whether the goal is to gain respect as a leader, achieve a higher education, or persuade a company to use a service, using correct grammar can be the difference between success and failure. This includes the proper use of vocabulary, punctuation, and standard grammar rules such as subject and verb agreement. The goal of all communication is to be comprehensible; proper grammar is a crucial step in reaching this goal. When grammatical errors such as these are made during verbal communication, the audience stops listening to the message and focuses on the mistake.

Parts of Speech

- Noun
  - Countable
    - Proper Noun
    - Common Noun
  - Uncountable
    - Abstract Noun
    - Collective Noun

NOUN

Definition: **a person, place or thing** is known as a noun. Here are some examples:

- **person**: man, woman, teacher, John, Mary
- **place**: home, office, town, countryside, America
- **thing**: table, car, banana, money, music, love, dog, monkey

Ways of recognizing a noun in a sentence:

1. Ending
2. Position
3. Function

1. Noun Ending: There are certain word endings that show that a word is a noun, for example:

- ity > nationality
- ment > appointment
- ness > happiness
- -ation > relation
- hood > childhood

But this is not true for the word endings of all nouns. For example, the noun "spoonful" ends in-ful, but the adjective "careful" also ends in -full.

2. Position in Sentence: We can often recognize a noun by its position in the sentence.

Nouns often come after a determiner (a determiner is a word like a, an, the, this, my, such):

- a relief
- an afternoon
- the doctor
- this word
- my house
- such stupidity

Nouns often come after one or more adjectives:

- a great relief
- a peaceful afternoon
- the tall, Indian doctor
- this difficult word
- my brown and white house
- such crass stupidity

3. Function in a Sentence: Nouns have certain functions (jobs) in a sentence, for example:

- Subject of verb: Doctors work hard.
- Object of verb: He likes coffee.
- Subject and object of verb: Teachers teach students.

But the subject or object of a sentence is not always a noun. It could be a pronoun or a phrase. In the sentence "My doctor works hard", the noun is "doctor" but the subject is "My doctor".

Classifications of Nouns

A. Noun can be classified as:

I. Proper Noun II. Common Noun

I. Proper Nouns: Proper nouns are a special type of names. In fact, when someone asks us our name, it is such a type of name we use in reply, i.e. Rajesh or Mohandas or Tina or any such name.

Some examples of proper nouns are:

- Names of people — Ram, Manoj;
- Brand names — like Pantaloon, Tata Indica, Lux or Dell;
- Geographical names — Asia, River Nile, Mount Everest, the Himalayas;
- Names of institutions — St. Michael's School, Bank of England, European Union;
- Names of books and films — Utopia, Wings of Fire, My Fair Lady.

II. Common Nouns: Common nouns are the general, unspecific categories of entities. Whereas Maharashtra is a proper noun because it signifies a specific state, the word state itself is a common noun because it can refer to any of the 28 states in India. They are names which are general in nature, not specific or unique names.

They can be:

- Names of people — man, woman, child, boy, girl (not Jai, Rajesh, Anita, Dolly);
- Names of animals — dog, cat, elephant (not Jackey, Rani or Jumbo);
- Names of places — city, village, river, mountain, country (not Dehradun, Kurumannu, River Indus or Mount Everest);
- Names of things — soap, apple, chair, aeroplane (not Lux, Golden Delicious, Neelkamal or Boeing).

Types of Common Noun

Common nouns are again of two types:

Countable nouns: These are nouns that can be counted (e.g. student, teacher, book, chair, city, and village). These nouns are names of people, places, things that we can count. If you put the numerals one, two, three, etc. before these nouns, they sound normal to people who know English very well. (e.g. one book, two villages, seven dwarfs.)

So, book, villages, dwarfs, men and countries are count nouns.

For example, the noun bike is countable noun. Consider the following sentence:

There is a bike in that garage.

In this example, the word bike is singular as it refers to one bike that is presently residing in a particular garage.

However, bike can also occur in the plural form.

There are six bikes in that garage.

In this example, the noun bikes refer to more than one bike as it is being modified by the numeral six.

Uncountable Nouns: These cannot be counted (e.g. milk, water, furniture, gold, wood, glass, work, information).

Countable Nouns

Uncountable Nouns

These nouns are not countable and are called uncountable nouns. For example, the word clutter is an uncountable noun.

That garage is full of clutter.

This sentence makes grammatical sense. However, the following example does not.

That garage is full of clutters.

These nouns cannot take plural forms, and therefore a sentence containing the word clutters is grammatically wrong.

Substances, liquids, and powders are entities that are often signified by uncountable nouns such as wood, sand, water, and flour.

3. **Collective Nouns:** Collective nouns are nouns that refer to a group of something in a specific manner. Given below are some examples of collective nouns. They are names of collections.
   - a crowd
   - a range of mountains
   - a deck of cards
   - a pile of books
   - an anthology of poems
   - a bunch of grapes
   - a pack of wolves
   - a swarm of bees
   - a network of computers
   - a host of golden daffodils

- a colony of ants live in the anthill
- The colored words in the above phrases are collective nouns.

4. **Abstract Nouns:** More ethereal, theoretical concepts use abstract nouns to refer to them. Words like freedom, love, power, and redemption are all examples of abstract nouns.

They hate us for our freedom. All you need is love. We must fight the power.

SOLVED EXERCISE

Q.1: What is a Noun?

Sol.: A noun is a word used to name a person, animal, place, thing, and abstract idea. Nouns are usually the first words which small children learn. The highlighted words in the following sentences are all nouns:

Late last year our neighbours bought a goat.

Portia White was an opera singer.

The bus inspector looked at all the passengers' passes.

According to Plutarch, the library at Alexandria was destroyed in 48 B.C.

Philosophy is of little comfort to the starving.

Q.2: What is Possessive Nouns?

Sol.: In the possessive case, a noun or pronoun changes its form to show that it owns or is closely related to something else. Usually, nouns become possessive by adding a combination of an apostrophe and the letter "s."

The red suitcase is Cassandra's.

The only luggage that was lost was the prime minister's.

You can form the possessive case of a singular noun that ends in "s" by adding an apostrophe alone or by adding an apostrophe and "s," as in the following examples:

The bus's seats are very uncomfortable.

The bus' seats are very uncomfortable.

The film crew accidentally crushed the platypus's eggs.

The film crew accidentally crushed the platypus' eggs.

Felicia Hemans's poetry was once more popular than Lord Byron's.

Felicia Hemans' poetry was once more popular than Lord Byron's.

You can form the possessive case of a plural noun that does not end in "s" by adding an apostrophe and a "s," as in the following examples:

The children's mittens were scattered on the floor of the porch.

The sheep's pen was mucked out every day.

Since we have a complex appeal process, a jury's verdict is not always final.

The men's hockey team will be playing as soon as the women's team is finished.

The hunter followed the moose's trail all morning but lost it in the afternoon.

You can form the possessive case of a plural noun that does end in "s" by adding an apostrophe:

The concert was interrupted by the dogs' barking, the ducks' quacking, and the babies' squalling.

The janitors' room is downstairs and to the left.

My uncle spent many hours trying to locate the squirrels' nest.

The archivist quickly finished repairing the diaries' bindings.

Religion is usually the subject of the roommates' many late night debates.

Q.3: What are different Types of Nouns?

Sol.: There are many different types of nouns. As you know, you capitalize some nouns, such as "Canada" or "Louise," and do not capitalize others, such as "badger" or "tree" (unless they appear at the beginning of a sentence). In fact, grammarians have developed a whole series of noun types, including the proper noun, the common noun, the concrete noun, the abstract noun, the countable noun (also called the count noun), the non-countable noun (also called the mass noun), and the collective noun. You should note that a noun will belong to more than one type: it will be proper or common, abstract or concrete, and countable or non-countable or collective.

Q.4: What is Proper Noun?

Sol.: You always write a proper noun with a capital letter, since the noun represents the name of a specific person, place, or thing. The names of days of the week, months, historical documents, institutions, organizations, religions, their holy texts and their adherents are proper nouns. A proper noun is the opposite of a common noun.

In each of the following sentences, the proper nouns are highlighted:

Beltane is celebrated on the first of May.

Abraham appears in the Talmud and in the Koran.

Q.5: What is Abstract Noun?

Sol.: An abstract noun is a noun which names anything which you can not perceive through your five physical senses, and is the opposite of a concrete noun. The highlighted words in the following sentences are all abstract nouns:

Justice often seems to slip out of our grasp.

Some scientists believe that schizophrenia is transmitted genetically.

Q.6: What is Collective Noun?

Sol.: A collective noun is a noun naming a group of things, animals, or persons. You could count the individual members of the group, but you usually think of the group as a whole is generally as one unit. You need to be able to recognise collective nouns in order to maintain subject-verb agreement. A collective noun is similar to a non-countable noun, and is roughly the opposite of a countable noun.

In each of the following sentences, the highlighted word is a collective noun:

The flock of geese spends most of its time in the pasture.

The collective noun "flock" takes the singular verb "spends."

The jury is dining on take-out chicken tonight.

EXERCISE

Q.1. What is a Noun?

Q.2. What is Possessive Nouns?

Q.3. What are different Types of Nouns?

Q.4. What is Collective Noun?

Q.5. What is Abstract Noun?

CHAPTER-2

Verb

Verbs are a necessary component of all sentences. It is a part of speech that expresses existence, action, or occurrence.

A **verb**, is a word derived from the Latin word ***verbum*** which means word, that conveys action (bring, read, walk, run, murder), or a state of being (exist, stand).

A **verb** is defined as **a word which shows action or state of being**. The verb is the heart of a sentence as every sentence must have a verb.

E.g. In the sentence The dog bit the man, bit is the *verb* as it is the word which shows the action of the sentence.

In the sentence: The man is sitting on a chair, even though the action doesn't show much activity, sitting is the *verb* of the sentence.

In the sentence: She is a smart girl, there is no action but a state of being expressed by the verb is. The word be is different from other *verbs* in many ways but can still be thought of as a *verb*.

Let's look at a few more examples:

1. Rahul ran into the burning building.
2. The beagle **stepped** on its ears.

In the above sentences, Rahul ran and the beagle stepped. Both show *action*.

Some verbs don't show action. Instead, they **link** the subject to some other information: these are called, linking verbs. Common linking verbs are "to be" forms—such as, **is, am, are, was, were**—and the verbs **appear, become, feel, look, seem.** Examples are:

1. She **was** fond of her animals.
2. She **looks** like she has been in a fight with a cat.
3. It **feels** damp in the grass.

In identifying the verb, you also need to look for the helpers, since they are considered part of the verb. The helpers (auxiliaries) include: *is, am, are, was, were, been, has, have, had, do, does, did, may, can, might, shall, will, should, could, would.*

Complete verb have been marked in the following:

1. He **should have let** me out of the house.
2. I **tried** to wait for him to get up.
3. He **should** not **have stayed** in bed so long.

Words with to in front of them are never a part of the verb, even though they look suspiciously like verbs. Words like not, always, just, never, and only are not part of the verb.

Sentence can also have more than one verb. One other thing: no word with an "-ing" ending can ever be the verb without a helper: I barking; she running?

Unlike most of the other parts of speech, verbs change their form. Sometimes endings are added (learn - learned) and sometimes the word itself becomes different (teach-taught). The different forms of verbs show different meanings related to such things as tense (past, present and future); person (first person, second person, third person), number (singular, plural) and voice (active, passive). Verbs are also often accompanied by verb-like words called modals (may, could, should, etc.) and auxiliaries (do, have, will, etc.) to give them different meanings.

Types of Verbs

English verbs are divided into three groups: Normal Verbs, Non-Continuous Verbs, and Mixed Verbs.

1. **Normal Verbs:** Most verbs are "Normal Verbs." These verbs are usually physical actions which you can see somebody doing. These verbs can be used in all tenses. e.g. to run, to walk, to eat, to fly, to go, to say, to touch, etc.

   Examples:

   - I **eat** dinner every day.
   - I **am eating** dinner now.

2. **Non-Continuous Verbs:** These verbs are usually things you cannot see somebody doing. These verbs are rarely used in continuous tenses. They include:

   - **Abstract Verbs** to be, to want, to cost, to seem, to need, to care, to contain, to owe, to exist...
   - **Possession Verbs** to possess, to own, to belong...
   - **Emotion Verbs** to like, to love, to hate, to dislike, to fear, to envy, to mind...

   Examples:

   - He **is needing** help now. ***Not Correct***
   - He **needs** help now. ***Correct***

- He **is wanting** a drink now. ***Not Correct***
- He **wants** a drink now. ***Correct***

3. **Mixed Verbs:** These verbs have more than one meaning. In a way, each meaning is a unique verb. Some meanings behave like "Non-Continuous Verbs," while other meanings behave like "Normal Verbs." e.g. to appear, to feel, to have, to hear, to look, to see, to weigh.

List of Mixed Verbs with Examples and Definitions:

To appear:

- Donna **appears** confused. *Non-Continuous Verb* DONNA SEEMS CONFUSED.
- My favorite singer **is appearing** at the jazz club tonight. *Normal Verb*
- MY FAVORITE SINGER IS GIVING A PERFORMANCE AT THE JAZZ CLUB TONIGHT.

To have:

- I **have** a rupee now. *Non-Continuous Verb I* POSSESS A RUPEE NOTE.
- I **am having** fun now. *Normal Verb I* AM EXPERIENCING FUN NOW.

To hear:

- She **hears** the music. *Non-Continuous Verb She hears the music with her ears.*
- She **is hearing** voices. *Normal Verb She hears something others cannot hear. She is hearing voices in her mind.*

To look:

- Nancy **looks** tired. *Non-Continuous Verb* SHE SEEMS TIRED.
- Farah **is looking** at the pictures. *Normal Verb* SHE IS LOOKING WITH HER *EYES.*

To miss:

- John **misses** Sally. *Non-Continuous Verb*
- Ge is sad because she is not there.
- Debbie **is missing** her favorite TV program. *Normal Verb*
- She is not there to see her favorite program.

To see:

- I **see** her. *Non-Continuous Verb*

  I see her with my eyes.
- I **am seeing** the doctor. *Normal Verb*

  I am visiting or consulting with a doctor. (Also used with dentist and lawyer.)
- I **am seeing** her. *Normal Verb*

  I am having a relationship with her.
- He **is seeing** ghosts at night. *Normal Verb*

He sees something others cannot see. For example ghosts, aura, a vision of the future, etc.

To smell:

- The coffee **smells** good. *Non-Continuous Verb*
  The coffee has a good smell.
- I **smell** the flowers. *Normal Verb*
  I am sniffing the flowers to see what their smell is like.

To taste:

- The coffee **tastes** good. *Non-Continuous Verb*
  The coffee has a good taste.
- I **taste** the cake. *Normal Verb*
  I am trying the cake to see what it tastes like.

To think:

- He **thinks** the test is easy. *Non-Continuous Verb*
  He considers the test to be easy.
- She **is thinking** about the question. *Normal Verb*
  She is pondering the question, going over it in her mind.

To weigh:

- The table **weighs** a lot. *Non-Continuous Verb*
  The table is heavy.
- She **is weighing** herself. *Normal Verb*
  She is determining her weight.

To feel:

- The massage **feels** great. *Non-Continuous Verb*
  The massage has a pleasing feeling.
- I **don't feel** well today. *Sometimes used as Non-Continuous Verb*
  I am a little sick.
- I **am not feeling** well today. *Sometimes used as Normal Verb*
  I am a little sick.

Verb with different Tenses

One of the most important things about *verbs* is their relationship to time. *Verbs* tell if something has already happened, if it will happen later, or if it is happening now. For things happening now, we use the present tense of a verb; for something that has already happened, we use the past tense; and for something that will happen later, we use the future tense. Some examples of *verbs* in each tense are in the chart below:

Present	Past	Future
Look	Looked	will look
Move	Moved	will move
Talk	Talked	will talk

Verbs like those in the chart above that form the past tense by adding -d or -ed are called **regular verbs**. Some of the most common verbs are not regular and the different forms of the verb must be learned. Some examples of such **irregular verbs** are in the chart below:

Present	Past	Future
See	Saw	will see
Hear	Heard	will hear
Speak	Spoke	will speak

The charts above show the simple tenses of the verbs. There are also progressive or continuous forms which show that the action takes place over a period of time, and perfect forms which show completion of the action. These forms will be discussed more in other lessons, but a few examples are given in the chart below:

Present Continuous	Present Perfect
is looking	has looked
is speaking	has spoken
is talking	has talked

The chart below showing verb with different tenses:

Simple Present	*Simple Past*	*Simple Future*
I study English every day.	Two years ago, I studied English in England.	If you are having problems, I will help you study English. I am going to study French next year.
Present Continuous	**Past Continuous**	**Future Continuous**
I am studying English now.	I was studying English when you called yesterday.	I will be studying English when you arrive tonight. I am going to be studying French when you arrive tonight.
Present Perfect	**Past Perfect**	**Future Perfect**
I have studied English in several different countries.	I had studied a little English before I moved to the U.K.	I will have studied every tense by the time I finish this course.

		I am going to have studied every tense by the time I finish this course.
Present Perfect Continuous	**Past Perfect Continuous**	**Future Perfect Continuous**
I have been studying English for five years.	I had been studying English for five years before I moved to the U.K.	I will have been studying English for over two hours by the time you arrive. I am going to have been studying French for over two hours by the time you arrive.

Regular Verbs List

There are thousands of regular verbs in English. Note that there are some spelling variations in American English (for example, "practice" becomes "practice" in American English).

- accept
- add
- admire
- admit
- advise
- afford
- back
- bake
- balance
- ban
- bang
- bare
- bat
- bathe
- calculate
- call
- camp
- care
- carry
- carve
- cause
- challenge
- allow
- amuse
- analyze
- announce
- annoy
- answer
- beg
- behave
- belong
- bleach
- bless
- blind
- blink
- blot
- choke
- chop
- claim
- clap
- clean
- clear
- clip
- close
- applaud
- appreciate
- approve
- argue
- arrange
- arrest
- boil
- bolt
- bomb
- book
- bore
- borrow
- bounce
- bow
- compare
- compete
- complain
- complete
- concentrate
- concern
- confess
- confuse
- attach
- attack
- attempt
- attend
- attract
- avoid
- brake
- branch
- breathe
- bruise
- brush
- bubble
- bump
- burn
- cough
- count
- cover
- crack
- crash
- crawl
- cross
- crush

- dam
- damage
- dance
- dare
- decay
- earn
- educate
- embarrass
- face
- fade
- fail
- fancy
- fasten
- gather
- gaze
- glow
- glue
- hammer
- hand
- handle
- hang
- happen
- harass
- identify
- ignore
- imagine
- impress
- jail
- jam
- kick
- kill
- label
- land
- last
- man
- manage
- march
- mark
- marry

- deliver
- depend
- describe
- desert
- deserve
- end
- enjoy
- enter
- fetch
- file
- fill
- film
- fire
- grab
- grate
- grease
- greet
- harm
- hate
- haunt
- head
- heal
- heap
- increase
- influence
- inform
- inject
- jog
- join
- kiss
- kneel
- learn
- level
- license
- matter
- measure
- meddle
- melt
- memorize

- disapprove
- disarm
- discover
- dislike
- divide
- excite
- excuse
- exercise
- flash
- float
- flood
- flow
- flower
- grin
- grip
- groan
- guarantee
- heat
- help
- hook
- hop
- hope
- hover
- intend
- interest
- interfere
- interrupt
- joke
- judge
- knit
- knock
- lighten
- like
- list
- milk
- mine
- miss
- mix
- moan

- dress
- drip
- drop
- drown
- drum
- explain
- explode
- extend
- force
- form
- found
- frame
- frighten
- guard
- guess
- guide
- hug
- hum
- hunt
- hurry
- invite
- irritate
- itch
- juggle
- jump
- knot
- load
- lock
- long
- move
- muddle
- mug
- multiply
- murder

- nail
- name
- obey
- object
- observe
- pack
- paddle
- paint
- park
- part
- pass
- question
- race
- radiate
- rain
- raise
- reach
- sack
- sail
- satisfy
- save
- saw
- scare
- scatter
- scold
- scorch
- scrape
- scratch
- scream
- screw
- talk
- tame
- tap
- taste
- undress
- unfasten
- vanish
- need
- nest
- obtain
- occur
- offend
- permit
- phone
- pick
- pinch
- pine
- place
- queue
- refuse
- regret
- reign
- reject
- rejoice
- shiver
- shock
- shop
- shrug
- sigh
- sign
- signal
- sin
- sip
- ski
- skip
- slap
- slip
- thaw
- tick
- tickle
- tie
- unite
- unlock
- visit
- nod
- note
- offer
- open
- order
- pop
- possess
- post
- pour
- practise
- pray
- remove
- repair
- repeat
- replace
- reply
- soothe
- sound
- spare
- spark
- sparkle
- spell
- spill
- spoil
- spot
- spray
- sprout
- squash
- squeak
- trace
- trade
- train
- transport
- unpack
- untidy
- notice
- number
- overflow
- owe
- own
- prevent
- prick
- print
- produce
- program
- promise
- rhyme
- rinse
- risk
- rob
- rock
- stop
- store
- strap
- strengthen
- stretch
- strip
- stroke
- stuff
- subtract
- succeed
- suck
- suffer
- suggest
- trot
- trouble
- trust
- try
- use

- wail
- wait
- walk
- wander
- x-ray
- yawn
- waste
- watch
- water
- wave
- yell
- whirl
- whisper
- whistle
- wink
- work
- worry
- wrap
- wreck

Irregular Verbs

Irregular verbs are an important feature of English. We use irregular verbs a lot when speaking, less when writing. Of course, the most famous English verb of all, the verb "to be", is irregular.

Subject Verb Agreement

Simple present tense verbs have a special form for the third person singular. Singular means "one" and plural means "more than one." A verb must "agree" with its subject. Subject-verb agreement generally means that the third person singular verb form must be used with a third person subject in the simple present tense. The word be - the most irregular and also most common verb in English-has different forms for each person and even for the simple past tense.

Person is used here to show who or what does the action and can have the following forms:

1st person or the self (I, we)

2nd person or the person spoken to (you)

3rd person or a person not presents (he, she, it, and they)

The third person singular forms are represented by the pronouns he, she, it. The chart below shows how the third person singular verb form changes:

Number	*Person*	*Present*	*Past*	*Future*
Singular	1st (I)	am	was	will be
	2nd (you)	are	were	will be
	3rd (he, she, it)	is	was	will be
Plural	1st (we)	are	were	will be
	2nd (you)	are	were	will be
	3rd (they)	are	were	will be

Usually a subject comes before a verb and an object may come after it. The subject is what does the action of the verb and the object is what receives the action. In the sentence Bobby ate a burger, Bobby is the subject or the one who did the eating and the burger is the object or what got eaten. A verb which has an object is called a transitive verb and some examples are throw, buy, hit, love. A verb which has no object is called an intransitive verb and some examples are go, come, walk, listen.

The future forms, use the word will and the perfect forms use the word have. These words are called helping or auxiliary verbs. The word be can serve as an auxiliary and will and shall are also auxiliary forms. The chart below shows two other verbs which can also be used as auxiliaries:

Number	*Person*	*Present*	*Past*
Singular	1st (I)	have	had
		do	did
	2nd (you)	have	had
		do	did
	3rd (he, she, it)	has	had
		does	did
Plural	1st (we)	have	had
		do	did
	2nd (you)	have	had
		do	did
	3rd (they)	have	had
		do	did

There is a type of auxiliary verb called a modal which changes the meaning of a verb in different ways.

Basic Principle of Subject Verb Agreement:

Singular subjects need singular verbs; plural subjects need plural verbs. My brother is a nutritionist. My sisters are mathematicians.

The indefinite pronouns anyone, everyone, someone, no one, nobody are always singular and, therefore, require singular verbs.

- Everyone has done his or her homework.
- Somebody has left her purse.

Some indefinite pronouns such as all, some are singular or plural depending on what they're referring to. Be careful choosing a verb to accompany such pronouns.

- Some of the beads are missing.
- Some of the water is gone.
- The mayor, who has been convicted along with his four brothers on four counts of various crimes but who also seems, like a cat, to have several political lives, is finally going to jail.

On the other hand, there is one indefinite pronoun, none, that can be either singular or plural; it often doesn't matter whether you use a singular or a plural verb unless something else in the sentence determines its number.

- None of you claim responsibility for this incident?
- None of the students have done their homework.

Everyone and Everybody

Some indefinite pronouns are particularly troublesome everyone and everybody certainly feel like more than one person and, therefore, students sometimes use a plural verb with them. They are always singular, though. Each is often followed by a prepositional phrase ending in a plural word (Each of the cars), thus confusing the verb choice. Each, too, is always singular and requires a singular verb.

I. Everyone has finished his or her homework.

II. You would always say, "Everybody is here."

This means that the word is singular and nothing will change that.

Each of the students is responsible for doing his or her work in the library.

Phrases such as together with, as well as, and along with are not the same as and. The phrase introduced by as well as or along with will modify the earlier word (mayor in this case), but it does not compound the subjects (as the word and would do).

- The mayor as well as his brothers is going to prison.
- The mayor and his brothers are going to jail.

The pronouns neither and either are singular and require singular verbs even though they seem to be referring, in a sense, to two things.

- Neither of the two traffic lights is working.
- Which shirt do you want for Christmas? Either is fine with me.

The conjunction or does not conjoin (as and does): when nor or or is used the subject closer to the verb determines the number of the verb. Whether the subject comes before or after the verb doesn't matter; the proximity determines the number.

- Either my father or my brothers are going to sell the house.
- Neither my brothers nor my father is going to sell the house.
- Are either my brothers or my father responsible?
- Is either my father or my brothers responsible?

Because a sentence like "Neither my brothers nor my father is going to sell the house" sounds peculiar, it is probably a good idea to put the plural subject closer to the verb whenever that is possible.

Verbs in the present tense for third-person, singular subjects (he, she, it and anything those words can stand for) have s-endings. Other verbs do not add s-endings.

He loves and she loves and they love and . . . .

Some words end in "s" and appear to be plural but are really singular and require singular verbs.

- Measles is a dangerous disease for pregnant women.

On the other hand, some words ending in "s" refer to a single thing but are nonetheless plural and require a plural verb.

- My assets were wiped out in the depression.
- The average worker's earnings have gone up dramatically.
- Our thanks go to the workers who supported the union.

The names of sports teams that do not end in "s" will take a plural verb: the Miami Heat have been looking ...,

Words such as glasses, pants, pliers, and scissors are regarded as plural (and require plural verbs) unless they're preceded the phrase pair of (in which case the word pair becomes the subject).

- My pants were torn.
- A pair of plaid trousers is in the closet.

Fractional expressions such as half of, a part of, a percentage of, a majority of are sometimes singular and sometimes plural, depending on the meaning. The same is true when all, any, more, most and some act as subjects. Sums and products of mathematical processes are expressed as singular and require singular verbs. The expression "more than one" (oddly enough) takes a singular verb: "More than one student has tried this."

- Some of the voters are still angry.
- A large percentage of the older population is voting against her.
- Two-fifths of the troops were lost in the battle.
- Two-fifths of the vineyard was destroyed by fire.
- Forty percent of the students are in favor of changing the policy.
- Forty percent of the student body is in favor of changing the policy.
- Two and two is four.
- Four times four divided by two is eight.

EXERCISES

Q.1 For each of the following sentences, fill in the blank with either the singular or the plural verb form shown in brackets.

- The committee ____ put forward a new proposal. (has, have)
- The committee ____ disagreed on what policy to adopt. (has, have)
- Two tons of coal __ required. (is, are)

ANSWERS

1. The committee has put forward a new proposal.

   The committee is acting as a whole. Therefore a singular verb is used.

2. The committee have disagreed on what policy to adopt.

   The members of the committee are acting as individuals. Therefore a plural verb is used.

3. Two tons of coal is required.

   The amount two tons is considered as a whole. Therefore a singular verb is used.

Q.2 Fill in the blanks with correct form of verb

1. The crew ______ preparing the ship to go to sea. (Is, are)
2. The crew ______ different levels of experience. (Has, have)
3. Two pounds of butter _____ too much. (Is, are)
4. The class _____ not agree on what should be done. (Does, do)
5. The class _____ contributed eighty dollars to the cause. (Has, have)
6. Three ounces of gold _____ worth more than three ounces of copper. (is, are)
7. The group _____ decided to hold a meeting once a month. (Has, have)
8. The group _____ varied backgrounds. (Has, have)
9. Fifty cents _____ the regular price. (Was, were)
10. Six dollars _____ been collected. (Has, have)

CHAPTER-3

Adverb

An **adverb** is a word that tells us more about a verb. **An adverb gives more information about a verb, an adjective or another adverb. Adverbs describe verbs, adjectives and adverbs in terms of such qualities as time, frequency and manner.** (The man ran **quickly**). But adverbs can also modify adjectives (Tara is **really** beautiful), or even other adverbs (It works **very** well).

Adverbs typically answer questions such as how? in what way?, when? where? and to what extent? In English, they often end in "ly". This function is called the adverbial function, and is realized not just by single words (i.e. adverbs) but by adverbial phrases and adverbial clauses.

Kinds of Adverb

Many different kinds of word are called adverbs. We can usually recognize an adverb by it's:

1. **Function**
2. **Form**
3. **Position**

1. **Function:** The principal job of an adverb is to describe verbs, adjectives and other adverbs. In the following examples, the adverb is in **bold** and the word that it modifies is in *italics*.
   - Modify a verb:
     - Neha *speaks* **loudly**. (How does John speak?)
     - Mary *lives* **locally**. (Where does Mary live?)
     - She **never** *smokes*. (When does she smoke?)
   - Modify an adjective:
     - He is **really** *handsome*.
   - Modify another adverb:
     - She drives **incredibly** *slowly*.

Other functions of Adverb:

- Modify a whole sentence:
  - **Obviously**, *I can't know everything.*
- Modify a prepositional phrase:
  - It's **immediately** *inside the door.*

2. **Form:** Many adverbs end in "ly". We form such adverbs by adding "ly" to the adjective. Here are some examples:
   - quickly, softly, strongly, honestly, interestingly

But not all words that end in "ly" are adverbs. "Friendly", for example, is an adjective.

Some adverbs have no particular form, for example:

- well, fast, very, never, always, often, still

3. **Position:** Adverbs have three main positions in the sentence:
   - Front (before the subject):
     - **Now** we will study nouns.
   - Middle (between the subject and the main verb):
     - We **often** study adverbs.
   - End (after the verb or object):
     - We study adverbs **carefully**.
   - Adverbs of Manner
   - She moved slowly and spoke quietly.
4. **Adverbs of Place:** This shows where an action or something is done or happens. It answers the question "Where?" Such adverbs are placed after the verb.
   - She has lived on the island all her life.
   - She still lives there now.
   - We met her in the zoo.
5. **Adverbs of Frequency:** This answers the question "How often?" Adverbs of frequency are very important because we often use them. Examples of these adverbs include: never, rarely, seldom, hardly ever, occasionally, sometimes, generally, usually, frequently, nearly always, often and ever. Also included are: quite, just, already, almost and nearly.
   - She takes the boat to the mainland every day.
   - She often goes by herself.
   - He will never have finished in time.
   - Jane is rarely late for work.

- Peter seldom reads the Bible.
- Sue hardly ever wore lipstick.

6. **Adverbs of Time:** This shows when an action or something is done or happens. It answers the question "When?" It is either placed at the beginning or at the end of a sentence. When they are at the beginning, they are often emphasized.
   - She tries to get back before dark.
   - It's starting to get dark now.
   - She finished her tea first.
   - She left early.
7. **Adverbs of Purpose:**
   - She drives her boat slowly to avoid hitting the rocks.
   - She shops in several stores to get the best buys.
8. **Adverbs of manner**: This shows how an action or something is done. It answers the question "How?" The adverb is placed just after the verb when it is used in a sentence.
   - Solemnly the minister addressed her congregation.
   - The minister solemnly addressed her congregation.
   - The minister addressed her congregation solemnly.
   - She cried loudly.
9. **Adverbs of Degree:** Adverbs of degree tell us about the intensity or degree of an action, an adjective or another adverb. Common adverbs of degree: ***Almost, nearly, quite, just, too, enough, hardly, scarcely, completely, very, extremely.***

   Adverbs of degree are usually placed:
   1. Before the adjective or adverb they are modifying:

      e.g. The water was ***extremely cold.***
   2. Before the main verb:

      e.g. He was ***just*** leaving. She has ***almost*** finished.

Examples:

- She doesn't ***quite*** know what she'll do after university.
- They are ***completely*** exhausted from the trip.
- I am ***too*** tired to go out tonight.
- He ***hardly*** noticed what she was saying.

Enough, very, too: Enough as an adverb meaning 'to the necessary degree' goes *after* adjectives and adverbs.

Example:

- Is your coffee ***hot enough***? (adjective)
- He didn't work ***hard enough***. (adverb)

It also goes before nouns and means 'as much as is necessary'. In this case it is not an adverb, but a 'determiner'.

Example:

- We have ***enough bread***.
- They don't have ***enough food***.

Too as an adverb meaning 'more than is necessary or useful' goes *before* adjectives and adverbs, e.g.

- This coffee is ***too*** hot. (adjective)
- He works ***too*** hard. (adverb)

Enough and **too** with adjectives can be followed by *'for someone/something'*.

Example:

- The dress was big ***enough*** for me.
- She's not experienced ***enough*** for this job.
- The coffee was ***too*** hot for me.
- The dress was ***too*** small for her.

We can also use *'to + infinitive'* after **enough** and **too** with adjectives/adverb.

Example:

- The coffee was ***too*** hot to drink.
- He didn't work hard ***enough*** to pass the exam.
- She's not old ***enough*** to get married.
- You're ***too*** young to have grandchildren.

Very goes before an adverb or adjective to make it stronger.

Example:

- The girl was ***very*** beautiful. (adjective)
- He worked ***very*** quickly. (adverb)

If we want to make a negative form of an adjective or adverb, we can use a word of opposite meaning, or ***not very***.

Example:

- The girl was ugly **OR** The girl was ***not very*** beautiful.
- He worked slowly **OR** He did***n't*** work ***very*** quickly.

There is a big difference between **too** and **very**.

- **Very** expresses a **fact**.

- He speaks ***very*** quickly.
- **Too** suggests there is a **problem**.

He speaks ***too*** quickly (*for me to understand).*

EXERCISES

Q.1 Pick out the adverbs from the following sentence and identify its kind.

1. We reached the place very early.
2. We have never met before.
3. He has to do it.
4. The teacher has gone out for a walk.
5. I met her a few minutes ago.
6. I am very happy to meet you.
7. She will travel on Friday.
8. She talks pleasingly.
9. I am quite sure that I will get through in my test.
10. She is too short.

Q.2 Fill in the blanks with suitable adverbs from the list given below. The kind of adverb that can be used is indicated in the brackets. Note that the same adverb can be used more than once.

Absolutely, quite, today, where too, now, patiently, often, therefore, freely, seldom, pleasantly, yesterday, why, quietly, enough

1. I am not .... sure. (Adverb of Degree)
2. You will .... see an image. (Adverb of Time)
3. He worked diligently and .... (Adverb of Manner)
4. We .... go skiing. (Adverb of Frequency)
5. You are .... right. (Adverb of Degree)
6. He .... comes here. (Adverb of frequency)
7. I have not seen him .... (Adverb of time)
8. He did not work hard ....he failed. (Adverb of reason)
9. She mingles ....with others. (Adverb of manner)
10. Are you ....prepared? (Adverb of manner)
11. I went to see her .... (Adverb of time)
12. I know the place .... he lives. (Relative adverb)
13. .... did you break my window? (Interrogative adverb)
14. That was ....he hit back. (Interrogative adverb)

15. He walked in .... (Adverb of manner)
16. I was ....surprised. (Adverb of manner)
17. I am ....weak to move about. (Adverb of degree)
18. He solved the problem quickly ....to pass the test. (Adverb of degree)

ANSWERS

1. I am not quite sure.
2. You will now see an image.
3. He worked diligently and patiently.
4. We seldom go skiing.
5. You are absolutely right.
6. He often comes here.
7. I have not seen him today.
8. He did not work hard, therefore he failed.
9. She mingles freely with others.
10. Are you quite prepared?
11. I went to see her yesterday.
12. I know the place where he lives.
13. Why did you break my window?
14. That was why he hit back.
15. He walked in quietly.
16. I was pleasantly surprised.
17. I am too weak to move about.
18. He solved the problem quickly enough to pass the test.

CHAPTER-4

Adjectives

Adjectives are words that describe or modify another person or thing in the sentence. Example of adjectives:

- a six-year-old child
- the unhappiest, richest man

DEGREES OF ADJECTIVES

The degrees of comparison are known as the positive, the comparative, and the superlative. We use the comparative for comparing two things and the superlative for comparing three or more things. Notice that the word than frequently accompanies the comparative and the word that precedes the superlative. The inflected suffixes -er and -est suffice to form most comparatives and superlatives, although we need -ier and -iest when a two-syllable adjective ends in y (happier and happiest); otherwise we use more and most when an adjective has more than one syllable.

Positive	*Comparative*	*Superlative*
Rich	Richer	Richest
lovely	Lovelier	Loveliest
beautiful	more beautiful	most beautiful

Certain adjectives have irregular forms in the comparative and superlative degrees:

Irregular Comparative and Superlative Forms

Good	Better	Best
Bad	Worse	Worst
Little	Less	Least
muchmanysome	More	Most
far	Further	Furthest

Kinds of Adjectives

There are different kinds of adjectives.

Adjectives of quality

Adjectives of quality describe the kind, quality or characteristic of a person, animal, place or thing.

She is a **brilliant** student.

He is an **honest** man.

Adjectives formed from proper nouns are also called adjectives of quality. Examples are: **Persian** carpets, **Indian** flag, **British** parliament, etc.

Adjectives of quantity

Adjectives of quantity describe **how much** of a thing is meant. Examples are: some, any, little, enough, all, much, etc.

He drank **all** the milk.

Is there **any** milk in the bottle?

Adjectives of Number

Adjectives of number indicate **how many** persons or things are meant. Examples are: few, many, several, two, five, second, fifth, etc.

Two girls came.

She is the **first** woman to climb Mt. Everest.

Distributive adjectives

Each, every, either and **neither** are called distributive adjectives.

She had a child hanging onto **each** hand.

I have invited **every** friend I have.

Demonstrative adjectives

This, that, these and **those** are called demonstrative adjectives.

Bring me **that** chair.

Who is **this** girl?

Those mangoes are all ripe.

Interrogative adjectives

Interrogative adjectives are used with nouns to ask questions. Examples are: **which, what, whose** etc.

Which shirt shall I buy?

Whose son is he?

Possessive adjectives

Possessive adjectives indicate possession. Examples are: my, his, her, our, their, your, its.

He is **my** father.

She is **our** teacher.

Is this **your** bag?

Less versus Fewer

When we compare quantities we often use the words *fewer* and *less*. Generally, when we're talking about countable things, we use the word *fewer*; when we're talking about measurable quantities that we cannot count, we use the word *less*. "She had fewer chores, but she also had less energy."

We do, however, definitely use *less* when referring to statistical or numerical expressions:

- It's less than twenty miles to Dallas.
- He's less than six feet tall.

In these situations, it's possible to regard the quantities as *sums* of countable measures.

I or me

When we make a comparison with "than" do we end with a subject form or object form, "taller than I/she" or "taller than me/her." The correct response is "taller than I/she." We are looking for the subject form:

"He is taller than I am/she is tall." (Except we leave out the verb in the second clause, "am" or "is"). If we can say "He is tall like me/her," then (if "than" could be prepositional like "*like*") we should be able to say, "He is taller than me/her." We also want to be careful in a sentence such as "I like him better than she/her." The "she" would mean that you like this person better than she likes him; the "her" would mean that you like this male person better than you like that female person.

EXERCISE

Q.1 A list of words is given below. Find out which among them are adjectives.
Clever, hot, cried, pleasant, brightly, efficiently, attractive, often, honesty, brilliance, efficiency, stopped, acted, smooth, quality, brave

ANSWERS

Clever, hot, pleasant, attractive, smooth, brave

EXERCISE

Q.1 What are the different types of adjective?

Q.2 A list of words is given below. Find out which among them are adjectives.
Clever, dry, hot, fat, golden, good, heavy, square, thin, small, naughty, pain, lane, bag, book, school

Q.3 Explain difference between
- Demonstrative adjectives
- Interrogative adjectives
- Adjectives of quality

CHAPTER-5

Punctuation

Punctuation is the use of standard marks and signs in writing to separate words into sentences, clauses, and phrases in order to clarify meaning. The marks or signs are called punctuation marks. Punctuation marks are signals to readers. When you speak, you can pause, stop, or change your tone of voice to make your meaning clear. You cannot do this when you write. When writing, you must use punctuation marks such as commas and question marks to make your meaning clear.

The use of punctuation marks can be very complex. Each punctuation mark can be used in many ways. Here are the punctuation marks that are most commonly used when writing and the most typical way or ways they are used.

Full stop (Period)

We use a **period [.]** at the end of a sentence that makes a statement. There is no space between the last letter and the period.

Use a period at the end of a **command**:

- Hand in the poster essays no later than noon on Friday.
- In case of tremors, leave the building immediately.

Use a period at the end of an **indirect question**:

- The teacher asked why Maria had left out the easy exercises.
- My father used to wonder why Manish's ears were so big.

Use a period with **abbreviations**:

Dr. Das arrived from Washington, D.C., at 6 p.m.

Notice that when the period ending the abbreviation comes at the end of a sentence, it will also suffice to end the sentence. On the other hand, when an abbreviation ends a question or exclamation, it is appropriate to add a question mark or exclamation mark after the abbreviation-ending period:

Did you enjoy living in Washington, D.C.?

Question Mark (?)

A **question mark is used** at the end of a direct question.

A **question** tag is a device used to turn a statement into a question. It nearly always consists of a pronoun, a helping verb, and sometimes the word *not*. Although it begins as a statement, the tag question prevails when it comes to the end-mark i.e. a question mark. Notice that when the statement is positive, the tag question is expressed in the negative; when the statement is negative, the tag question is positive. There are a few exceptions to this, frequently expressing an element of surprise or sarcasm: "So you've made your first million, have you? The following are more typical tag questions:

- He should quit smoking, shouldn't he?
- He shouldn't have quit his diet, should he?

(Be careful of this last one; it's not "weren't they?")

We need *not* to put a question mark at the end of an **indirect question**.

- The instructor asked the students what they were doing.
- I asked my sister if she had a date.

Be careful to distinguish between an indirect question (above), and a question that is embedded within a statement which we *do* want to end with a question mark.

- We can get to Boston quicker, can't we, if we take the interstate?
- His question was, can we end this statement with a question mark?

Sometimes a question will actually end with **a series of brief questions**. When that happens, especially when the brief questions are more or less follow-up questions to the main question, each of the little questions can begin with a lowercase letter and end with a question mark.

- Who is responsible for executing the plan? The coach? The coaching staff? The players?

If a question mark is part of an **italicized or underlined title**, make sure that the question mark is also italicized:

- My favorite book is *Where Did He Go?*
- Did he sing the French national anthem, *la Marseillaise*?

When a question ends with an abbreviation, end the abbreviation with a period and then add the question mark.

- Didn't he use to live in Washington, D.C.?

When a question constitutes a **polite request**, it is usually *not* followed by a question mark. This becomes more true as the request becomes longer and more complex:

- Would everyone in the room who hasn't received an ID card please move to the front of the line.

Exclamation Mark. (!)

An **exclamation mark is used** at the end of an emphatic declaration, interjection, or command.

"No!" he yelled. "Do it now!"

An exclamation mark may be used to close questions that are meant to convey extreme emotion, as in

What on earth are you doing! Stop!

An exclamation mark can be inserted within parentheses to emphasize a word within a sentence.

We have some really (!) low-priced rugs on sale this week.

Note that there is no space between the last letter of the word so emphasized and the parentheses. This device should be used rarely, if ever, in formal text.

An exclamation mark will often accompany mimetically produced sounds, as in

"All night long, the dogs *woof!* in my neighbor's yard"

"The bear went *Grr!*, and I went left."

We do not add a period after such a sentence that ends with the title's exclamation mark. The exclamation mark will also suffice to end the sentence.

Colon (:)

A **colon is used** before a list or an explanation that is preceded by a clause that can stand by itself.

We will often use a colon to separate an independent clause from a quotation that the clause introduces:

The acting director often used her favorite quotation from Shakespeare's *Tempest*: "We are such stuff as dreams are made on; and our little life is rounded with a sleep."

With today's sophisticated word-processing programs (which know how much space to put after punctuation marks), we insert only one space (hit the space-bar only once) after a colon.

It might be useful to say, also, when we <u>don't</u> use a colon. Remember that the clause that precedes the mark (where you're considering a colon) ought to be able to stand on its own as an independent clause. Its purpose might be strictly to introduce the clause that follows, so it might feel rather incomplete by itself, but grammatically it will have both a subject and a predicate. In other words, we would <u>not</u> use a colon in situations like the following:

- Her usual advice, I remember, was "Keep your head up as you push the ball up the court." (no colon after "was")

If the independent clause coming after the colon is a formal quote, begin that quoted language with a capital letter.

Whitehead had this to say about writing style: "Style is the ultimate morality of mind."

If the explanatory statement coming after a colon consists of more than one sentence, begin the independent clause immediately after the colon with a capital letter:

There were two reasons for a drop in attendance at NBA games this season: First, there was no superstar to take the place of Michael Jordan. Second, fans were disillusioned about the misbehavior of several prominent players.

If the introductory phrase preceding the colon is very brief and the clause following the colon represents the real business of the sentence, begin the clause after the colon with a capital letter:

Remember: Many of the prominent families of this New England state were slaveholders prior to 1850.

If the function of the introductory clause is simply to introduce, and the function of the second clause (following the colon) is to express a *rule,* begin that second clause with a capital:

Let us not forget this point: Appositive phrases have an entirely different function than participial phrases and must not be regarded as dangling modifiers.

Semicolon (;)

I have grown fond of semicolons in recent years. . . . It is almost always a greater pleasure to come across a semicolon than a period. The period tells you that that is that; if you didn't get all the meaning you wanted or expected, anyway you got all the writer intended to parcel out and now you have to move along. But with a semicolon there you get a pleasant little feeling of expectancy.

— *Lewis Thomas*

Semicolon is used

To separate closely related independent clauses:

My grandmother seldom goes to bed this early; she's afraid she'll miss out on something.

The semicolon allows the writer to imply a relationship between nicely balanced ideas without actually stating that relationship. (Instead of saying *because* my grandmother is afraid she'll miss out on something, we have implied the *because.* Thus the reader is involved in the development of an idea—a clever, subliminal way of engaging the reader's attention.)

It is rare, but certainly possible, that you will want a semicolon to separate two independent clauses even when those two independent clauses are connected by a coordinating conjunction. This is especially true when the independent clauses are complex or lengthy and when there are commas within those independent clauses. You might consider breaking those two independent clauses into separate sentences when this happens.

- Coach Auriemma realized that his next recruiting class contained two superb guards, a fine post player, and a power forward; but as of the end of the spring recruiting season, he was still pushing to discover better first-year players for the interior positions.

The Hyphen

Hyphens have other uses

(*a*) creating compound words, particularly modifiers before nouns
e.g. the well-known actor, my six-year-old daughter, the out-of-date curriculum

(*b*) writing numbers twenty-one to ninety-nine and fractions
e.g. five-eighths, one-fourth

(*c*) creating compounds on-the-fly for fly-by-night organizations

(*d*) Adding certain prefixes to words: When a prefix comes before a capitalized word or the prefix is capitalized, use a hyphen (non-English, A-frame, I-formation). The prefixes *self-*, *all-*, and *ex-* nearly always require a hyphen e.g. ex-husband, all-inclusive, self-control, and when the prefix ends with the same letter that begins the word, you will often use a hyphen e.g. anti-intellectual, de-emphasize, but not always (unnatural, coordinate, cooperate). There is no space between a hyphen and the character on either side of it.

Suspended Compounds

With a series of nearly identical compounds, we sometimes delay the final term of the final term until the last instance, allowing the hyphen to act as a kind of place holder, as in

- The third- and fourth-grade teachers met with the parents.
- Both full- and part-time employees will get raises this year.
- We don't see many 3-, 4-, and 5-year-old children around here.

Dash

Use a **dash** [—] (or two hyphens [—] on old-fashioned typewriters) or **dashes** as a super-comma or set of super-commas to set off parenthetical elements, especially when those elements contain internal forms of punctuation:

e.g. All four of them—Bob, Jeffrey, Jason, and Brett—did well in college.

Do not use dashes to set apart material when commas would do the work for you. Usually, there are no spaces between the dash and the letters on either side of a dash.

In writing dialogue, the dash is used to show breaks in thought and shifts in tone:

"How many times have I asked you not to —" Jai suddenly stopped talking and looked out the window.

"Not to do what?" I prompted.

"Not to — Oh heck, I forget!"

A dash is sometimes used to set off concluding lists and explanations in a more informal and abrupt manner than the colon. Modern word processors provide for two kinds of dashes: the regular dash or em dash (which is the same width as the letter "M," —) and the en dash (which is about half the width, the same as the letter "N," –). We use the dash for most purposes and keep its smaller brother, the en dash, for marking the space between dates in a chronological range: "Kennedy's presidency (1961–1963) marked an extraordinary era. . . ."; in time: 6:30–8:45 p.m.; and between numbers and letters in an indexing scheme: table 13–C, CT Statute 144–A.

Parentheses [( )]

We use **parentheses** to include material that you want to de-emphasize or that wouldn't normally fit into the flow of your text but you want to include nonetheless. If the material within parentheses appears within a sentence, do not use a capital letter or full stop to punctuate that material, even if the material is itself a complete sentence. If the material within your parentheses is written as a separate sentence (not included within another sentence), we have to punctuate it as if it were a separate sentence.

- Thirty-five years after his death, Robert Frost (we remember him at Kennedy's inauguration) remains America's favorite poet.
- Thirty-five years after his death, Robert Frost (do you remember him?) remains America's favorite poet.
- Thirty-five years after his death, Robert Frost remains America's favourite poet. (We remember him at Kennedy's inauguration.)

If the material is important enough, use some other means of including it within your text. Parentheses tend to de-emphasize text whereas dashes tend to make material seem even more important.

Bracket

Brackets are used in the following situations:

To include explanatory words or phrases within quoted language:

Lew Perkins, the Director of Athletic Programs, said that Pumita Espinoza, the new soccer coach [at Notre Dame Academy] is going to be a real winner.

If you are quoting material and you've had to change the capitalization of a word or change a pronoun to make the material fit into your sentence, enclose that changed letter or word(s) within brackets:

Esha charged her former employer with "falsification of [her] coaching record."

It was the *atmosphere* of the gym that thrilled Jacobs, not the eight championship banners hanging from the beams.

You can use brackets to include parenthetical material inside parenthetical material:

Chernwell was poet laureate of Bermuda (a largely honorary position [unpaid]) for ten years.

Be kind to your reader, however, and use this device sparingly.

The Apostrophe **[']**

WE USE AN **APOSTROPHE** TO CREATE POSSESSIVE FORMS, CONTRACTIONS, AND SOME PLURALS. The apostrophe shows where a letter or letters have been left out of a **contracted verb:**

I am = I'm	you are = you're	she is = she's	it is = it's
do not = don't	she would = she'd	he would have = he would've	
let us = let's	who is = who's	she will = she'll	they had = they'd

Paraphrasing

Nowadays paraphrasing is widely used in teaching. Teachers like to use this technique to explain complex sentences or words so that they can help their students better understand those language points. Students are required to master this technique because paraphrase is one of their test programs. Paraphrasing is based on understanding. Without through understanding, right paraphrasing is hard to achieve. However, understanding is only the first step for paraphrasing. The second step is expressing. Right expressing is not only based on right understanding. Therefore, by doing paraphrasing, students can practice and improve their comprehension and expression capability.

Paraphrasing involves putting a passage from source material into your own words. A paraphrase must also be attributed to the original source. Paraphrased material is usually shorter than the original passage, taking a somewhat broader segment of the source and condensing it slightly.

Paraphrasing means "repeating or restating what another person says or what a text says in other words." The objective of paraphrasing is to make the listener or the other person understand that you have completely comprehended the matter. Paraphrasing is used effectively in teaching and learning to clarify a lot of concepts and principles. In customer service, paraphrasing on the part of the customer care executive makes the customer feel that his concerns are being understood are properly. He can then have the peace of mind that his grievances can be addressed well. Paraphrasing is different from parroting. In the latter, the exact words of the speaker are repeated, while in paraphrasing, the choice of words is different but the meaning conveyed is the same. Paraphrasing is sought to simplify a particular text or piece of information. Paraphrasing can be done through writing or in the form of speech.

The benefit of paraphrasing is that the speaker gets positive feedback and ensures that whatever he has spoken is being understood by the listener. This prompts the speaker to proceed further and stops him from repeating the same statement more than once.

Meaning of Paraphrasing

A paraphrase is when you write published materials in your own words without changing its original meaning. It is usually about the same length as the original, as opposed to a summary which is usually much shorter. It is important that the sentence structure and the vocabulary are not too similar to the original.

Purpose of Paraphrasing

Provide support for claims or add credibility to your writing

Give examples of several points of view on a subject

Call attention to a position that you wish to agree or disagree with

Highlight a particularly striking phrase, sentence, or passage by quoting the original

Expand the breadth or depth of your writing

Steps of Paraphrasing

Paraphrasing involves following steps:

- Read the entire text, noting the key points and main ideas.
- Summarize in your own words what the single main idea of the essay is.
- Paraphrase important supporting points that come up in the essay.
- Consider any words, phrases, or brief passages that you believe should be quoted directly.
- change the structure of the paragraph

- change the words.
- It is not enough to do just one of these; you need to change the structure and the words. You must do this to avoid plagiarism.
- Changing the structure of a paragraph
- Use the following steps to change the structure of a paragraph.
- Write down the main ideas & concepts
- Read the paragraph and write down the main points or words. Do not copy down entire sentences.
- Put the original away
- Put the paragraph / book away and using the main points, write your paraphrase from memory. This means that you are not copying the text word for word.
- Check your version against the original
- To avoid accidental plagiarism, check what you have written against the original text. You should check that they are not the same as well to see if you have left anything out.

Changing the words

People's writing styles and the words they use are very distinct. It is generally easy to tell when someone has copied directly from a textbook, as the language and the words used change from the writer's normal style and vocabulary. To paraphrase a text, follow these steps.

1. Read the sentence to be paraphrased a number of times.
2. Read the sentence / paragraph you want to paraphrase a number of times to get the meaning of the text. Once you understand it, write out the sentence in your own words. If you do not fully understand the text, do not attempt to paraphrase it, as you will just copy it.
3. Circle the specialized words, i.e. the words that the text is actually about. These will need to be included in your paraphrase, as without these words, the meaning of the paraphrase will change completely.
4. Underline the keywords that can be changed. You now have a starting point to construct your paraphrase.
5. Find other words and phrases that have similar meanings that can be used to replace the keywords in the text. Use a thesaurus or dictionary to help if need be.

The act of paraphrasing can help you to piece together seemingly disparate chunks of content into a coherent concept. Often the speaker's meaning will only became clear to you when you attempt to paraphrase it.

To prove to the other party that you truly do understand what they are saying. An interchangeable paraphrase is the only technique we know that will do this.

PARAPHRASING EXAMPLES

Original Paragraph: Example 1.

"Business communication is increasingly taking place internationally – in all countries, among all peoples, and across all cultures. An awareness of other cultures – of their languages, customs, experiences and perceptions – as well as an awareness of the way in which other people conduct their business, are now essential ingredients of business communication" (Chase, O'Rourke & Wallace, 2003, p.59).

Example of Paraphrasing

The importance of understanding the traditions, language, perceptions and the manner in which people of other cultures conduct their business should never be underestimated, and is a crucial component of business communication (Chase, O'Rourke & Wallace, 2003).

Summary Writing

Summarizing involves putting the main idea(s) into your own words, including only the main point(s). Once again, it is necessary to attribute summarized ideas to the original source. Summaries are significantly shorter than the original and take a broad overview of the source material.

EXERCISES

Now that you understand most of the rules of punctuation, you may like to test yourself by correcting the following sentences. The answers are given on the next page.

Q.1 The new regulations will prove to be to everyone's disadvantage.

Q.2 All of these books are to be catalogued the ones on geology natural history philosophy and scientific method.

Q.3 As well as being an excellent basketball player the girl was also a member of the winning squash team.

Q.4 The point is according to my understanding that we should move quickly.

Q.5 Instead Chambers 1988 suggests the importance of the genetic influence in determining the antecedents.

Q.6 It was found however that most of the liquid could not be absorbed.

Q.7 The miner his face covered in mud climbed slowly out.

Q.8 The trend toward specialization is very clear particularly in the professions.

Q.9 Once daylight came we thought we were safe however this was not to be.

Q.10 Keats poem 'To Autumn' is possibly the greatest evocation of that season ever written.

Q.11 After their long walk the boy's noses were red with cold.

Q.12 Its not easy to isolate its cause but we think its due to the torrential rain we had recently.

Q.13 The car left the road rolled down the bank turned over several times hit a free and then burst into flames.

Q.14 Gourmets and aren't we all gourmets will particularly enjoy the marinated quail.

Q.15 It was a rather hit or miss affair we found to our horror that we were expected to provide the entertainment as well.

ANSWERS TO EXERCISES

1. The new regulations will prove to be to everyone's disadvantage.
2. All of these books are to be catalogued: the ones on geology, natural history, philosophy and scientific method.
3. As well as being an excellent basketball player, the girl was also a member of the winning squash team.
4. The point is, according to my understanding that we should move quickly.
5. Instead, Chambers (1988) suggests the importance of the genetic influence in determining the antecedents.
6. It was found, however, that most of the liquid could not be absorbed.
7. The miner, his face covered in mud, climbed slowly out of the pit.
8. The trend toward specialization is very dear — particularly in the professions.
9. Once daylight came we thought we were safe; however, this was not to be.
10. Keats' poem 'To Autumn' is possibly the greatest evocation of that season ever written.
11. After their long walk the boys' noses were red with cold.

12. It's not easy to isolate its cause, but we think it's due to the torrential rain we had recently.
13. The car left the road, rolled down the bank, turned over several times, hit a tree, and then burst into flames.
14. Gourmets (and aren't we all gourmets?) will particularly enjoy the marinated quail.
15. It was a rather hit-or-miss affair; we found to our horror that we were expected to provide the entertainment as well!

CHAPTER-6

Essay Writing

An essay is usually a short piece of writing which is quite often written from an author's personal point of view. Essays can consist of a number of elements, including: literary criticism, political manifestos, learned arguments, observations of daily life, recollections, and reflections of the author. Few points are important while going for essay writing:

- Analyze
- Argue
- Compare and contrast
- Describe
- Discuss
- Summarize

Foundations to Effective Business Writing

The key to truly effective writing is being absolutely clear about what we want to say, what we want people to do, think or feel as a result of reading our writing.

Type-face lay out, choice of words, font-size, the use of BOLD or italics, grammar and spelling accuracy, quality of paper, etc, everything makes an impact upon the reader.

Steps of essay writing

1. **Organize Your Ideas:** Develop an outline to organize your ideas. An outline shows your main ideas and the order in which you are going to write about them. Write down all the main ideas.
2. List the subordinate ideas below the main ideas.
3. Avoid any repetition of ideas.

Structure of an essay

Every essay is made up of three parts:

1. Introduction
2. Body
3. Conclusion

Introduction

The introduction is the first paragraph of an essay. It often begins with a general statement about the topic and ends with a more specific statement of the main idea of your essay. The purpose of the introduction is to let the reader know what the topic is inform the reader about your point of view arouse the reader's curiosity so that he or she will want to read about your topic.

Body

- The body of an essay follows the introduction. It consists of a number of paragraphs in which you develop your ideas in detail.
- Limit each paragraph to one main idea.
- Prove your points continually by using specific examples and quotations.
- Use transition words to ensure a smooth flow of ideas from paragraph to paragraph.

Conclusion

The conclusion is the last paragraph of the paper. Its purpose is to summarize your main points, leaving out specific examples restate the main idea of the paper.

DIFFERENT TYPES OF ESSAYS

Narrative Essays

The first important thing to remember about a narrative essay is that it tells a story. This type of essays may be about an experience or event from past a recent or an ongoing experience or event something that happened to somebody else.

The second important thing about a narrative essay is that the story should have a point. In the final paragraph, the writer should come to an important conclusion about the experience that has just been described.

There are some guiding factors which must be remembered when choosing a narrative topic:

- An interesting plot should be planned.
- Some human characters should be involved.
- A certain amount of dialogue should be used.
- Choose a familiar setting. Your narration will become personal.
- Use your five senses freely to avoid vagueness.

Read this sample narrative essay, and then read the notes below.

"Learning something new can be a scary experience." This statement introduces the subject of the essay, which is a particular learning experience that the author had. The use of "I" in the essay indicates that what is being described is a personal experience.

The essay is essentially a story about something that happened. The author gives sufficient details about the people, place, and events so that the reader gets a clear idea of how the author feels about them. In the essay, the author "stood timidly" and the teacher "smiled" and was "patient." These words indicate the author's fears and the sense of security provided by the teacher who helped the author get over her fear.

In the final paragraph of the essay, the author reflects on the larger meaning or importance of the experience described. The author concludes that learning to swim has helped her to feel more confident about herself in other new situations. The idea that self-confidence comes from conquering your fears is something that all people can relate to. This is the point of the story.

The essay is well-organized. After the introduction, the author describes the experience as it happened in time — going to the pool the first day, having the first lesson, and the result of the subsequent lessons. The author might have chosen, however, to talk about the things she learned in order of their importance or difficulty.

The writing in an essay should be lively and interesting. Try to engage the reader's interest by adding details or personal observations. Sharing personal thoughts and details invites the reader into author's world and makes the story more personal and more interesting.

Descriptive Essays

The purpose of a descriptive essay is to describe a person, place, or thing in such vivid detail that the reader can easily form a precise mental picture of what is being written about. The author may accomplish this by using imaginative language, interesting comparisons, and images that appeal to the senses.

This type of essay requires a very careful and sensitive approach. All your senses must be used to make your description come alive and interest the reader. Consider the minor and significant details in persons, places and things. First write the general impression of the person, place or thing and thing and then go on to describe the details in order of importance.

A descriptive composition runs the maximum risk of becoming insipid. So, care should be given that a vivid description is always more interesting and readable than a dull lifeless one.

Read this sample descriptive essay, and then read the notes below.

The subject of the sample essay is fairly ordinary—a ride on a Ferris wheel. The author makes it interesting, however, by comparing the Ferris wheel to a monstrous creature.

The author makes good use of fresh and varied vocabulary. For example, in the first paragraph alone, she uses verbs that create excitement like "fascinate," "amaze," and "terrify." In the second paragraph she uses a variety of terms to describe the machine such as "monstrosity," "mythical beast," "amazing dinosaur," "fire-breathing dragon."

The author uses her senses to describe the scene—how the ride looks, sounds, smells, and feels. The ride is "huge, smoky, noisy" and its engines "drone" like the roar of a dragon. On the ride, she gets a "rush of adrenaline" and a "lump in her throat," she feels immobile and then weightless.

The essay is well organized. The introduction begins with a general statement, "I have always been fascinated by carnival rides," and ends with a more specific statement of what the essay will be about, "the thrill and excitement of a carnival ride keeps me coming back for more." The body of the essay is composed of several paragraphs that describe the Ferris wheel, the way it seems from the ground and the way it feels to ride on one. The conclusion restates the main idea of the essay that the author continues to find carnival rides thrilling and exciting.

Imaginative Essays

In this type you have to place yourself in the position of another person or object and narrate or describe:

- a story
- an autobiography
- a story with a given introduction/conclusion
- a story with given number of characters

'If I were ....' essays

Do not let your imagination get the better of you. We have to limit to the dimensions of the topic. Hence, sight of the topic should not be lost.

Remember some points while writing such essays:

Build a plan and stick to it.

Use your five senses imaginatively.

Build your characters with human qualities based on real life.

Do not turn characters into caricatures.

Be a habitual reader and learn to question the how, when, where and why of everything. It gives enough matter to build an essay.

Reflective Essays

In reflective essays first think about your subject as a whole and then unit by unit. Reflective essays mainly cover following topic:

- Habits, feelings, capacities
- Qualities, punctuality, heroism, patriotism
- Social, political, domestic and natural circles

You need to develop a main idea keeping in mind the impression you want to create. In these essays always maintain unity and do not allow irrelevant ideas to dominate your thinking.

Argumentative Essays

In this type of essay statements should be sensible and language should be clear. The opinions given in the essay must be balanced. The reader should be able to respect your judgement.

Some guiding points for argumentative essays:

- Always support your evidence with facts and figures.
- Place facts in order of importance.
- You should present constructive criticism.
- Do not make strong statements.
- Respect age, gender, party and profession.
- Consider both sides of the argument fairly and avoid controversy.

In essay writing always remembers do not work without a plan. Make clear cut units. Paragraph planning should be there. Essay writing strikes the right note and exhibits your mental organization and brain work.

1. Begin by introducing the debate topic in your own words.
2. Then write if you agree or disagree with the argument.
3. Tell people why you hold that opinion and come up with ideas and examples to back up your arguments. Try to put these ideas in an order with the most important ideas first and links between each idea so that the essay flows well.
4. Think about why people might have a different opinion (objections) and try to show why they are not important or they are not true.
5. Conclude with a brief summary and try to make a strong last sentence that people will remember. For example, Oprah Winfrey famously wrote," I believe the choice to be excellent begins with aligning your thoughts and words with the intention to require more from yourself." The rest of the article maybe forgotten, but that strong sentence is remembered.

Expository Essay

An exposition essay is one in which the main purpose of the paper is to explain something or to inform the reader about something. It is basically considered to be factual writing. This can be done in a number of ways; therefore, it is important to completely understand the purpose of the paper before writing it. Below are the different types of expository essays you might be asked to write. One type of exposition is the exemplification essay that uses examples to illustrate or explain something. Examples work best in an essay that is written to support something, clarify something, or to promote interest in a certain subject. They work well if you want to persuade the reader.

Process Analysis Essay

Another type of exposition essay is the process analysis essay. This essay explains the steps needed to complete a procedure, process, or particular task. This is often referred to as a "how to" essay. In this essay you must first identify materials or tools that are needed for the task, and then chronologically sequence the steps to be followed. You must explain the steps so that anyone reading the paper can successfully complete the procedure.

Compare/Contrast Essay

A third type of exposition essay is the compare and/or contrast essay. The thesis statement of this paper is how you feel about the subjects, and the body explains how you arrived at this opinion. This essay is written in two different patterns. The first pattern is point by point. In this format you compare the two subjects in each paragraph, using the points you are making about the subjects as the topic for each paragraph. You will have three body paragraphs, and both subjects will be mentioned in all three body paragraphs.

Thesis: A Ford is much better than a Chevrolet.

Point 1: Looks

A. Ford

B. Chevrolet

Point 2: Durability

A. Ford

B. Chevrolet

Point 3: Maintenance & Operating Costs

A. Ford

B. Chevrolet

Conclusion

In the block method, you will have a total of only four paragraphs, and you will make all points about the first subject in the first body paragraph and all the points about the second subject in the second body paragraph.

Thesis: A Ford is much better than a Chevrolet.

Subject 1: Ford

A. Looks

B. Durability

C. Maintenance and Operating Costs

Subject 2: Chevrolet

A. Looks

B. Durability

C. Maintenance and Operating Costs

Conclusion

These two formats are used whether you compare the two subjects, contrast the two subjects, or compare and contrast the two subjects.

Definition Essay

In a definition essay you give a clear and concise definition of the subject you are writing about, and then you develop the definition even further by giving examples.

Classification Essay

In a classification essay, you will group items or subjects into categories to help the reader better understand them. Make sure that your categories are distinct and separate, and make sure there is no overlapping of categories. You should introduce the idea with a definite purpose for classifying the information. Provide enough details to make each category clearly recognizable and make your paper interesting.

Cause and Effect Essay

When you are writing about why something happened or may happen, you are writing about causes and effects (results). The paper could be formatted to show that one cause has several different effects, or that several different causes result in one effect. When you report the conditions that produce one result, you are writing about causes resulting in one effect. When you talk about several results of one cause, you are writing about effects.

Cause (car emissions) Cause (factory smoke) effect (air pollution)

Cause (aerosol cans) effect (hole in ozone)

Cause (air pollution) effect (change in weather patterns) effect (acid rain)

You need to concentrate on either the causes or effects in your paper and clearly show how one relates to another.

EXERCISES

Q.1 Write essay on the following topics:

(*a*) Window shopping

(*b*) The attraction of Sundays

(*c*) A career in science attracts more boys than girls

(*d*) Advertising today

(*e*) Education should do more to prepare people for adult life.

Q.2 Explain difference between

(*a*) Process Analysis Essay and Compare/Contrast Essay

(*b*) Reflective Essays and Argumentative Essays

Q.3 Describe expository essays.

Q.4 Explain argumentative essays with the help of an example.

Q.5 How are imaginative and narrative essays different from each other?

CHAPTER-7

Basic Forms of Communication

Communication is a process of transferring information from one entity to another. Communication processes are sign-mediated interactions between at least two agents which share a repertoire of signs and semiotic rules. Communication is commonly defined as "the imparting or interchange of thoughts, opinions, or information by speech, writing, or signs". Although there is such a thing as one-way communication, communication can be perceived better as a two-way process in which there is an exchange and progression of thoughts, feelings or ideas (energy) towards a mutually accepted goal or direction (information).

Communication is a process whereby information is enclosed in a package and is channeled and imparted by a sender to a receiver via some medium. The receiver then decodes the message and gives the sender a feedback. All forms of communication require a sender, a message, and a receiver. Communication requires that all parties have an area of communicative commonality. There are auditory means, such as speech, song, and tone of voice, and there are nonverbal means, such as body language, sign language, paralanguage, touch, eye contact, through media, i.e., pictures, graphics and sound, and writing.

Why Study Communication?

- Knowing
  - o What happens when people communicate with themselves and others.
- Understanding
  - o How that knowledge can be used to explain and interpret the process of Communication in everyday life.
- Developing Skills
  - o Using this knowledge and understanding to communicate more effectively.
- The art of Communication is not all natural. We can learn to communicate effectively

- All Communication involves the creation and exchange of meanings via signs and symbols
- Communication Studies involves the business of making and understanding these signs and symbols
- People seem to have a real need to read meaning into all human action.

Forms and types of communication

Form of communication	*Example*	*Where/why important*
Verbal		
Nonverbal		
Graphic		
Type of communication		
Intrapersonal		
Interpersonal		
Public		
Mass		

Forms of communication

There is some degree of complexities for structuring who will communicate with whom. These systems of communication network regular patterns of person to person relationships through which information flows in an organization. Two kinds of networks exist: Formal and Informal. Formal Communication networks are system designed by management to dictate are so simple that they may hardly be notified; in a longer organization, they communication networks is with organization charts.

1st Downwards: Communication superior to subordinate.

Types: Job instruction rational for job organization procedure and practices, Feedback to subordinates indoctrination to organization culture.

2nd Upwards: Communication subordinate to superior.

Types: What subordinates doing unsolved problems, Suggestion for improvement, feeling about job and co-workers?

3rd Horizontal: communication between co-workers with different areas of responsibility.

Types: Coordinate tasks solve problems share information manage conflict build rapport.

Albert Mehrabian identified three major parts that convey meaning in human face to face communication: **body language, voice tonality, and words**. He conducted research to determine how people make meaning when a speaker says one thing but means another. If the speaker is sending a mixed message the listener will rely on the following cues to determine true meaning:

- 55% of impact is determined by body language—postures, gestures, and eye contact,
- 38% by the tone of voice, and
- 7% by the content or the words spoken.

Mehrabian says this only applies in situations where the speaker is talking about feelings or attitudes.

Although the exact percentage of influence may differ due to variables such as the perceptions or biases of the listener and the speaker, communication as a whole is meant to convey meaning and thus, in some cases, can be universal. A system of signals, such as voice sounds, intonations or pitch, gestures or written symbols can communicate thoughts or feelings. If a language employs communicating with signals, voice, sounds, gestures, or written symbols, can animal communications be considered to be a language? Animals do not have a written form of a language, but use a language to communicate with each another. In that sense, animal communication can be considered as a separate language.

Human spoken and written languages can be described as a system of symbols and the grammars by which the symbols are manipulated. The word "language" is also used to refer to common properties of languages. Language learning is normal in human childhood. Most human languages use patterns of sound or gesture for symbols which enable communication with others around them. There are thousands of human languages, and these seem to share certain properties, even though many shared properties have exceptions.

There is no defined line between a language and a dialect, but the linguist Max Weinreich is credited as saying that "a language is a dialect with an army and a navy". Constructed languages such as Esperanto, programming languages, and various mathematical formalisms are not necessarily restricted to the properties shared by human languages.

Bernard Luskin, 1970, advanced computer assisted instruction and began to connect media and psychology into what is now the field of media psychology. In 1998, the American Association of Psychology, Media Psychology Division 46 Task Force report on psychology and new technologies combined media and communication as pictures, graphics and sound increasingly dominate modern communication.

- **Verbal**
  - o Requires words
  - o May be speech or writing
    - § Conversation

§ Face-to-face
§ Telephone
§ Letter
§ Email
§ Text message
§ Fax
§ Messenger/chat

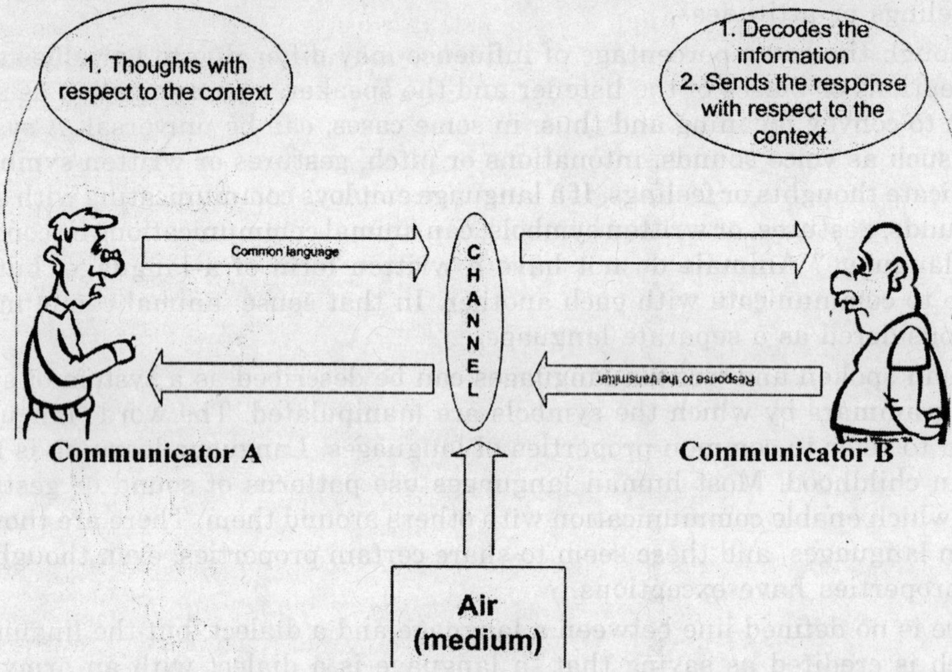

- The basis of communication is the interaction between people. Verbal communication is one way for people to communicate face-to-face. Some of the key components of verbal communication are sound, words, speaking, and language.
- At birth, most people have vocal cords, which produce sounds. As a child grows it learns how to form these sounds into words. Some words may be imitative of natural sounds, but others may come from expressions of emotion, such as laughter or crying. Words alone have no meaning. Only people can put meaning into words. As meaning is assigned to words, language develops, which leads to the development of speaking.
- The actual origin of language is subject to considerable speculation. Some theorists believe it is an outgrowth of group activities such as working together or dancing. Others believe that language developed from basic

sounds and gestures.

- Over 3,000 languages and major dialects are spoken in the world today. The development of languages reflects class, gender, profession, age group, and other social factors. The huge variety of languages usually creates difficulties between different languages, but even within a single language there can be many problems in understanding.
- Through speaking we try to eliminate this misunderstanding, but sometimes this is a very hard thing to do. Just as we assume that our messages are clearly received, so we assume that because something is important to us, it is important to others. As time has proven this is not at all true. Many problems can arise is speaking and the only way to solve these problems is through experience.
- Speaking can be looked at in two major areas: interpersonal and public speaking. Since the majority of speaking is an interpersonal process, to communicate effectively we must not simply clean up our language, but learn to relate to people.
- In interpersonal speaking, etiquette is very important. To be an effective communicator one must speak in a manner that is not offending to the receiver. Etiquette also plays an important role in an area that has developed in most all business settings: hierarchical communication. In business today, hierarchical communication is of utmost importance to all members involved.
- The other major area of speaking is public speaking. From the origin of time, it has been obvious that some people are just better public speakers than others. Because of this, today a good speaker can earn a living by speaking to people in a public setting. Some of the major areas of public speaking are speaking to, persuade, speaking to inform, and speaking to inspire or motivate.

Nonverbal communication

Nonverbal communication is the process of communicating through sending and receiving wordless messages. Such messages can be communicated through gesture, body language or posture; facial expression and eye contact, object communication such as clothing, hairstyles or even architecture, or symbols and info graphics, as well as through an aggregate of the above, such as behavioral communication. Nonverbal communication plays a key role in every person's day to day life, from employment to romantic engagements.

Speech may also contain nonverbal elements known as paralanguage, including voice quality, emotion and speaking style, as well as prosodic features such as rhythm, intonation and stress. Likewise, written texts have nonverbal elements such as handwriting style, spatial arrangement of words, or the use of emoticons. A portmanteau of the English words emotion and icon, an emoticon is a symbol or combination of symbols used to convey emotional content in written or message form.

Other communication channels such as telegraphy fit into this category, whereby signals travel from person to person by an alternative means. These signals can in themselves be representative of words, objects or merely be state projections. Trials have shown that humans can communicate directly in this way without body language, voice tonality or words.

Non-verbal is divided communication into four broad categories:

Physical: This is the personal type of communication. It includes facial expressions, tone of voice, sense of touch, sense of smell, and body motions.

Aesthetic: This is the type of communication that takes place through creative expressions: playing instrumental music, dancing, painting and sculpturing.

Signs: This is the mechanical type of communication, which includes the use of signal flags, the 21-gun salute, horns, and sirens.

Symbolic: This is the type of communication that makes use of religious, status, or ego-building symbols.

Static Features

Distance: The distance one stands from another frequently conveys a non-verbal message. In some cultures it is a sign of attraction, while in others it may reflect status or the intensity of the exchange.

Orientation: People may present themselves in various ways: face-to-face, side-to-side, or even back-to-back. For example, cooperating people are likely to sit side-by-side while competitors frequently face one another.

Posture: Obviously one can be lying down, seated, or standing. These are not the elements of posture that convey messages. Are we slouched or erect? Are our legs crossed or our arms folded? Such postures convey a degree of formality and the degree of relaxation in the communication exchange.

Physical Contact: Shaking hands, touching, holding, embracing, pushing, or patting on the back all conveys messages. They reflect an element of intimacy or a feeling of (or lack of) attraction.

Dynamic Features

Facial Expressions: A smile, frown, raised eyebrow, yawn, and sneer all convey information. Facial expressions continually change during interaction and are monitored constantly by the recipient. There is evidence that the meaning of these expressions may be similar across cultures.

Gestures: One of the most frequently observed, but least understood, cues is a hand movement. Most people use hand movements regularly when talking. While some gestures (e.g., a clenched fist) have universal meanings, most of the others are individually learned and idiosyncratic.

Looking: Major feature of social communication is eye contact, It can convey emotion, signal when to talk or finish, or aversion. The frequency of contact may suggest either interest or boredom.

Visual communication

Visual communication as the name suggests is communication through visual aid. It is the conveyance of ideas and information in forms that can be read or looked upon. Primarily associated with two dimensional images, it includes: signs, typography, drawing, graphic design, illustration, colour and electronic resources. It solely relies on vision. It is form of communication with visual effect. It explores the idea that a visual message with text has a greater power to inform, educate or persuade a person. It is communication by presenting information through visual form.

The evaluation of a good visual design is based on measuring comprehension by the audience, not on aesthetic or artistic preference. There are no universally agreed-upon principles of beauty and ugliness. There exists a variety of ways to present information visually, like gestures, body languages, video and TV. Here, focus is on the presentation of text, pictures, diagrams, photos, et cetera, integrated on a computer display. The term visual presentation is used to refer to the actual presentation of information. Recent research in the field has focused on web design and graphically oriented usability. Graphic designers use methods of visual communication in their professional practice.

Case Study

A German junior executive was unaware that he was making his team angry by seeming to be better than they were. They also saw him as self aggrandizing and aggressive.

Problem: He was up for a promotion, but no one wanted to work with him. We had to identify what words and what attitudes were annoying people and why.

Solution: He studied books (Carnegie, Covey) which talked about the ways people express themselves here in the US and what kind of vocabulary works. For instance, instead of saying "you are wrong" he found it more effective to say" what I think I heard you say is.... I don't know if I agree with you on that, can you explain more?" (See the article Dos and Don'ts in Corporate Meetings). We did role playing, going through hypothetical situations, and he practiced using the newly acquired vocabulary which he chose in order to not antagonize anybody yet still reflect his ideas, and get the results he wanted.

Results: He was promoted, and the training carried over to his personal and social life, where he was able to apply his new way of speaking very successfully. He felt much better about himself and he was happier with the way he fit into his surroundings.

EXERCISE

Q.1 What do you understand by communication?

Q.2 What do you different forms of communication?

Q.3 What is the meaning of non verbal communication?

Q.4 What do you understand by term visual communication.

Q.5 What are the forms (verbal, nonverbal and graphic) and types of communication (intrapersonal, interpersonal, public and mass). Use the drafted above to provide examples for each type and form of communication and where and/or why they are important.

Q.6 What might happen if the different forms of communication conflict? For example, it is often clear when a person is lying as the nonverbal communication betrays the verbal communication. Provide other examples of conflict between the different forms of communication and the subsequent effect on the communication message.

ESSENTIALS OF COMMUNICATION

Q.1 You have been assigned the job of composing business messages. What check-list would you prepare for organizing the message?

Ans. Check-list for organizing the message:

A. Organization:

1 Recognize good organization

(*a*) Subject and purpose are clear

(*b*) Information is directly related to subject and purpose.

(*c*) Ideas are grouped and presented logically

(*d*) All necessary information is included

2. Achieve good organization through outlining-

(*a*) Decide what to say

(*i*) Main idea

(*ii*) Major points

(*iii*) Evidence

(*b*) Organize the message to respond the audience is probable reaction-

(*i*) Use the direct approach when audience will be neutral, pleased, interested, or eager.

(*ii*) Use the indecent approach when audience will be displeased, interested, or unwilling.

3. Choose the appropriate organization plan-

(*a*) Short Messages:

(*i*) Direct request

(*ii*) Routine, good news and good message

(*iii*) Bad news message

(*iv*) Persuasive Message

(*b*) Longer message

(*i*) Information pattern (*ii*) Analytical pattern.

A. Formulation

1. Compose your first draft.

(*a*) Get ideas down as quickly as you can.

(*b*) Rearrange, delete, and add ideas without losing sight of your purpose.

2. Vary the style to create a tone that suits the occasion.

(*a*) Establish your relationship with your audience.

(*i*) Use the appropriate level of formality.

(*ii*) Avoid being overly familiar, using inappropriate humor, including obvious flattery, sounding preachy, bragging, and trying to be something you're not.

(*b*) Extend your audience-centered approach by using the "you" attitude.

(*c*) Emphasize the positive aspects of your message.

(*d*) Establish your credibility to gain the audience's confidences.

(*e*) Make your tone a polite one.

(*f*) Use the style that your company prefers.

Q. Explain clearly the advantages of a formal communication.(November-2008)

Ans. Communication is the principal means by which members of an organization work together. It helps to bind them together, enabling them to react to and influence each other.

Formal communication: A formal communication flows along prescribed channels which all organizational members desirous of communicating with one another are obliged to follow. Every organization has a built in hierarchal system that can he compared to a pyramid. It can, therefore, be understood that communication normally flows top downwards. But it is not always so. Communication in an organization is multidimensional and multidirectional.

Advantages of formal communication

(*a*) The formal channels account for most of the effectiveness of communication. Therefore, a great care has to he taken in sending across any letter or report through the proper formal channels.

(*b*) Formal channels cover an ever – widening distance as organization grows. Through them, it is easier to reach out to the branches of an organization spread far and wide.

(*c*) Formal channels, because of their tendency to filter information, keep the higher level managers from bogged down.

(*d*) Formal channels of communication consolidate the organization and satisfy the people in managerial position.

Q.8 What is meant by 'Critical thinking'? How shall you develop critical thinking? (November-2007)

Ans. Critical Thinking: Critical thinking is the discipline of rigorously and skillfully using information, experience, observation and reasoning to guide one's decisions, actions and beliefs. Critical thinking refers to the act of question of every step of the thinking process e.g. Have you considered all the facts? Have you tested your assumptions? Is your reasoning sound? Can you be sure your judgment is unbiased? Is your thinking process logical, rational and complete?

Developing Critical thinking: To develop as a critical thinker, one must be motivated to develop the following attributes:

1. **Open-minded:** Readiness to accept and explore alternative approaches and ideas.
2. **Well informed:** Knowledge of the facts and what is happening on all fronts.
3. **Experimental:** Thinking through 'what if scenarios to create probable options and then test the theories to determine what will work and what will not be acceptable.
4. **Contextual:** Keeping in mind the appropriate context in the course of analyses.

   Apply factors of analysis is that are relevant or appropriate.
5. **Reserved in making conclusion:** Knowledge of when, a conclusion is a 'fact' and when it is not only true conclusions support decisions.

Q.9 What is meant by "Active listening"? State the importance of 'Active listening' in the business communication skills. (June-2009)

Ans. Active Listening: Most of us assume that listening is a natural trait, but practically very few of us listen properly. What we regularly do is "we hear but do not listen". Hearing is through ears and listening is by mind. Listening happens when we understand and message as intended by sender. Many managers are so used to helping people solve problems that their first cause of action is transforming solutions and giving advice instead of listening with full attention directed towards understanding what the co-worker or staff member needs. Therefore, every employer and worker needs a listening ear.

If one does not learn how to listen, a great deal of what people are trying to tell you would be missed. In addition appropriate response would not be possible. Active listening is important for several reasons.

(*i*) It aids the organization in carrying out its missions.

(*ii*) It helps individuals to advance in their careers.

(*iii*) It provides information that helps them to learn about important happenings in the organization, as well as assisting them in doing their own jobs well.

(*iv*) It also helps in building strong personal relationships.

CHAPTER-8

Communication Models

A model is presentation of real phenomenon in abstract terms that can be applied in different forms at different times. Communication is an extremely complex process that becomes more complex with ever changing communication phenomenon. Complexities and constant changes in communication process make it imperative that it is presented in simple and generalized way to explain and understand the structure and function of communication. Communication model presents this simplification.

SHANNON'S MODEL OF THE COMMUNICATION PROCESS

Shannon's (1948) model of the communication process is, in important ways, the beginning of the modern field. It provided, for the first time, a general model of the communication process that could be treated as the common ground of such diverse disciplines as journalism, rhetoric, linguistics, and speech and hearing sciences. Part of its success is due to its structuralize reduction of communication to a set of basic constituents that not only explain how communication happens, but why communication sometimes fails. Good timing played a role as well. The world was barely thirty years into the age of mass radio, had arguably fought a world war in its wake, and an even more powerful, television, was about to assert itself. It was time to create the field of communication as a unified discipline, and Shannon's model was as good an excuse as any. The model's enduring value is readily evident in introductory textbooks. It remains one of the first things most students learn about communication when they take an introductory communication class. Indeed, it is one of only a handful of theoretical statements about the communication process that can be found in introductory textbooks in both mass communication and interpersonal communication.

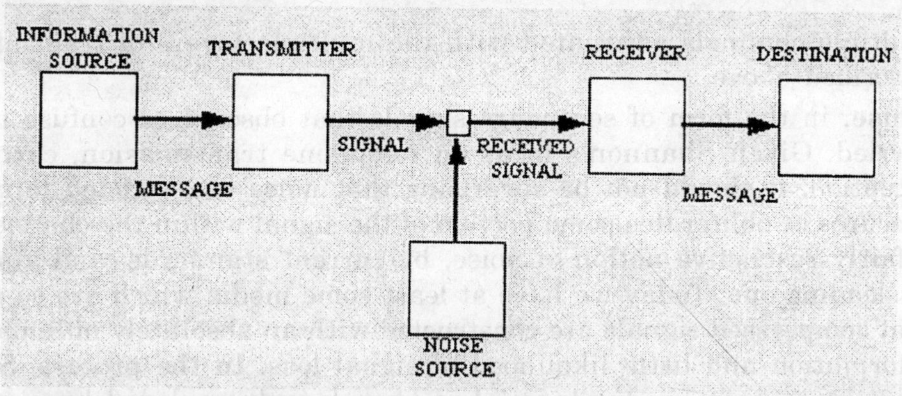

Fig.8.1: Shannon's (1948) Model of the communication process.

Shannon's model, as shown in Fig.8.1, breaks the process of communication down into eight discrete components:

1. An information **source**. Presumably a person who creates a message.
2. The **message**, which is both sent by the information source and received by the destination.
3. A **transmitter**. For Shannon's immediate purpose a telephone instrument that captures an audio signal, converts it into an electronic signal, and amplifies it for transmission through the telephone network. Transmission is readily generalized within Shannon's information theory to encompass a wide range of transmitters. Simplest transmission system that associated with face-to-face communication has at least two layers of transmission. The first, the mouth (sound) and body (gesture) create and modulate a signal. The second layer, which might also be described as a channel, is built of the air (sound) and light (gesture) that enable the transmission of those signals from one person to another. A television broadcast would obviously include many more layers, with the addition of cameras and microphones, editing and filtering systems, a national signal distribution network (often satellite), and a local radio wave broadcast antenna.
4. The **signal**, which flows through a channel. There may be multiple parallel signals, as is the case in face-to-face interaction where sound and gesture involve different signal systems that depend on different channels and modes of transmission. There may be multiple serial signals, with sound and/or gesture turned into electronic signals, radio waves, or words and pictures in a book.
5. A carrier or **channel**, which is represented by the small unlabeled box in the middle of the model. The most commonly used channels include air, light, electricity, radio waves, paper, and postal systems. Note that there may be

multiple channels associated with the multiple layers of transmission, as described above.

6. **Noise**, in the form of secondary signals that obscure or confuse the signal carried. Given Shannon's focus on telephone transmission, carriers, and reception, it should not be surprising that noise is restricted to noise that obscures or obliterates some portion of the signal within the channel. This is a fairly restrictive notion of noise, by current standards, and a somewhat misleading one. Today we have at least some media which are so noise free that compressed signals are constructed with an absolutely minimal amount information and little likelihood of signal loss. In the process, Shannon's solution to noise, redundancy, has been largely replaced by a minimally redundant solution: error detection and correction. Today we use noise more as a metaphor for problems associated with effective listening.
7. A **receiver**. In Shannon's conception, the receiving telephone instrument. In face to face communication a set of ears (sound) and eyes (gesture). In television, several layers of receiver, including an antenna and a television set.
8. A **destination**. Presumably a person who consumes and processes the message.

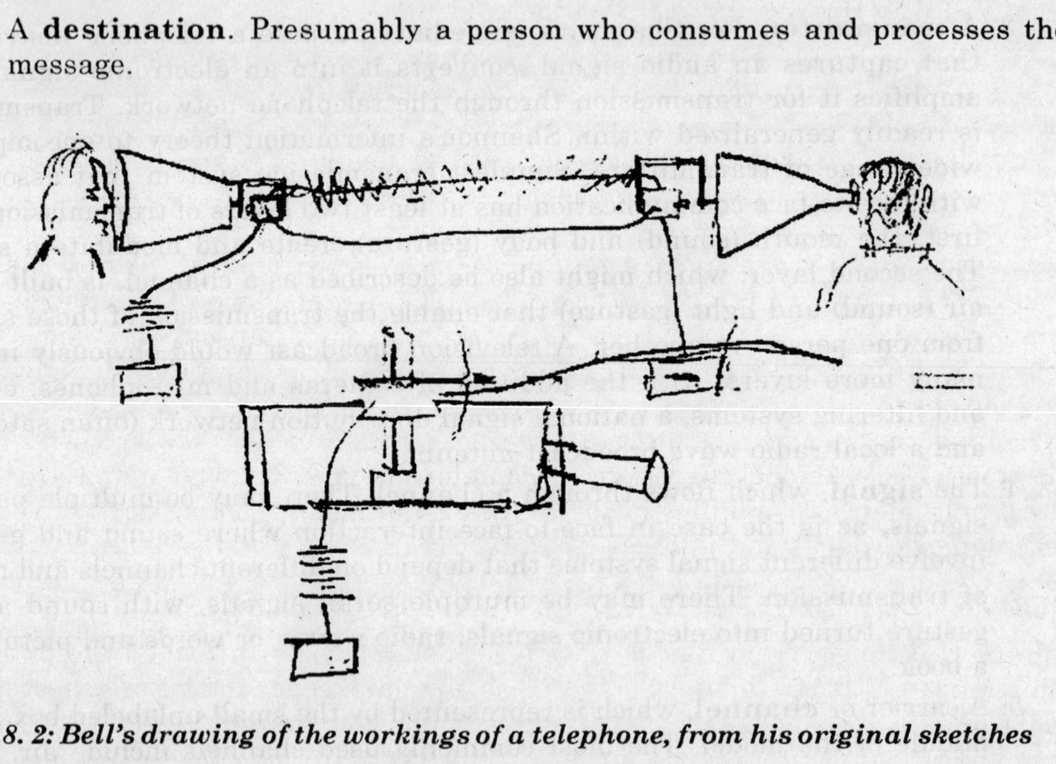

Fig.8. 2: Bell's drawing of the workings of a telephone, from his original sketches

Like all models, this is a minimalist abstraction of the reality it attempts to reproduce. The reality of most communication systems is more complex. Most information sources (and destinations) act as both sources and destinations. Transmitters, receivers, channels, signals, and even messages are often layered both serially and in parallel such that there are multiple signals transmitted and received, even when they are converged into a common signal stream and a common channel. Many other elaborations can be readily described.. It remains, however, that Shannon's model is a useful abstraction that identifies the most important components of communication and their general relationship to one another. That value is evident in its similarity to real world pictures of the designs of new communication systems, including Bell's original sketches of the telephone, as seen in Fig.8.2.

Bell's sketch visibly contains an information source and destination, transmitters and receivers, a channel, a signal, and an implied message (the information source is talking). What is new, in Shannon's model (aside from the concept of noise, which is only partially reproduced by Bell's batteries), is a formal vocabulary that is now generally used in describing such designs, a vocabulary that sets up both Shannon's mathematical theory of information and a large amount of subsequent communication theory. This correspondence between Bell's sketch and Shannon's model is rarely remarked (see Hopper, 1992 for one instance).

Shannon's model isn't really a model of communication, however. It is, instead, a model of the flow of information through a medium, and an incomplete and biased model that is far more applicable to the system it maps, a telephone or telegraph, than it is to most other media. It suggests, for instance, a "push" model in which sources of information can inflict it on destinations. In the real world of media, destinations are more typically self-selecting "consumers" of information who have the ability to select the messages they are most interested in, turn off messages that don't interest them, focus on one message in preference to other in message rich environments, and can choose to simply not pay attention. Shannon's model depicts transmission from a transmitter to a receiver as the primary activity of a medium. In the real world of media, messages are frequently stored for elongated periods of time and/or modified in some way before they are accessed by the "destination". The model suggests that communication within a medium is frequently direct and unidirectional, but in the real world of media, communication is almost never unidirectional and is often indirect.

DERIVATIVE MODELS OF THE COMMUNICATION PROCESS

One of these shortcomings is addressed in Fig.8.2's intermediary model of communication (sometimes referred to as the gatekeeper model or two-step flow (Katz, 1957)). This model, which is frequently depicted in introductory texts in mass communication, focuses on the important role that intermediaries often play in the communication process. Mass communication texts frequently specifically associate editors, who decide what stories, will fit in a newspaper or news broadcast, with this intermediary or gatekeeper role. There are, however, many intermediary roles (Foulger, 2002a) associated with communication. Many of these intermediaries have the ability to decide what messages others see, the context in which they are seen, and when they see them. They often have the ability, moreover, to change messages or to prevent them from reaching an audience (destination). In extreme variations we refer to such gatekeepers as censors. Under the more normal conditions of mass media, in which publications choose some content in preference to other potential content based on an editorial policy, we refer to them as editors (most mass media), moderators (Internet discussion groups), reviewers (peer-reviewed publications), or aggregators (clipping services), among other titles. Delivery workers (a postal delivery worker, for instance) also act as intermediaries, and have the ability to act as gatekeepers, but are generally restricted from doing so as a matter of ethics and/ or law.

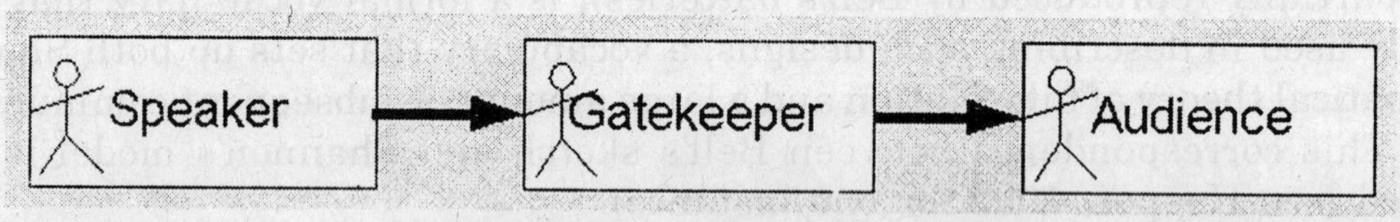

Fig.8. 3: An Intermediary Model

Variations of Fig.8.3's gatekeeper model are also used in teaching organizational communication, where gatekeepers, in the form of bridges and liaisons, have some ability to shape the organization through their selective sharing of information. These variations are generally more complex in depiction and often take the form of social network diagrams that depict the interaction relationships of dozens of people. They network diagrams often presume, or at least allow, bi-directional arrows such that they are more consistent with the notion that communication is most often bidirectional.

The bi-directionality of communication is commonly addressed in interpersonal communication text with two elaborations of Shannon's model (which is often labeled as the action model of communication): the interactive model and the transitive model. The interactive model, a variant of which is shown in Fig.8.4, elaborates Shannon's model with the cybernetic concept of feedback (Weiner, 1948, 1986), often (as is the case in Fig.8.4) without changing any other element of Shannon's model. The key concept associated with this elaboration is that destinations provide feedback on the messages they receive such that the information sources can adapt their messages, in real time. This is an important elaboration, and as generally depicted, a radically oversimplified one. Feedback is a message (or a set of messages). The source of feedback is an information source. The consumer of feedback is a destination. Feedback is transmitted, received, and potentially disrupt able via noise sources. None of this is visible in the typical depiction of the interactive model. This doesn't diminish the importance of feedback or the usefulness of elaborating Shannon's model to include it. People really do adapt their messages based on the feedback they receive. It is useful, however, to notice that the interactive model depicts feedback at a much higher level of abstraction than it does messages.

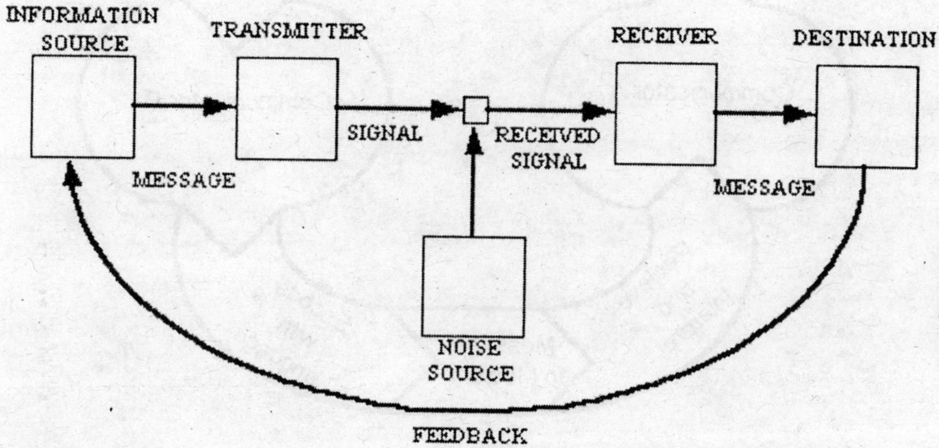

Fig.8.4: An Interactive Model

This difference in the level of abstraction is addressed in the transactional model of communication, a variant of which is shown in Fig.8.5. This model acknowledges neither creators nor consumers of messages, preferring to label the people associated with the model as communicators who both create and consume messages. The model presumes additional symmetries as well, with each participant creating messages that are received by the other communicator. This is, in many ways, an excellent model of the face-to-face interactive process which extends readily to any interactive medium that provides users with symmetrical interfaces for creation and consumption of messages, including notes, letters, C.B. Radio, electronic mail, and the radio. It is, however, a distinctly interpersonal model that implies an equality between communicators that often doesn't exist, even in interpersonal contexts. The caller in most telephone conversations has the initial upper hand in setting the direction and tone of a a telephone callr than the receiver of the call (Hopper, 1992).In face-to-face head-complement interactions, the boss (head) has considerably more freedom (in terms of message choice, media choice, ability to frame meaning, ability to set the rules of interaction) and power to allocate message bandwidth than does the employee (complement). The model certainly does not apply in mass media contexts.

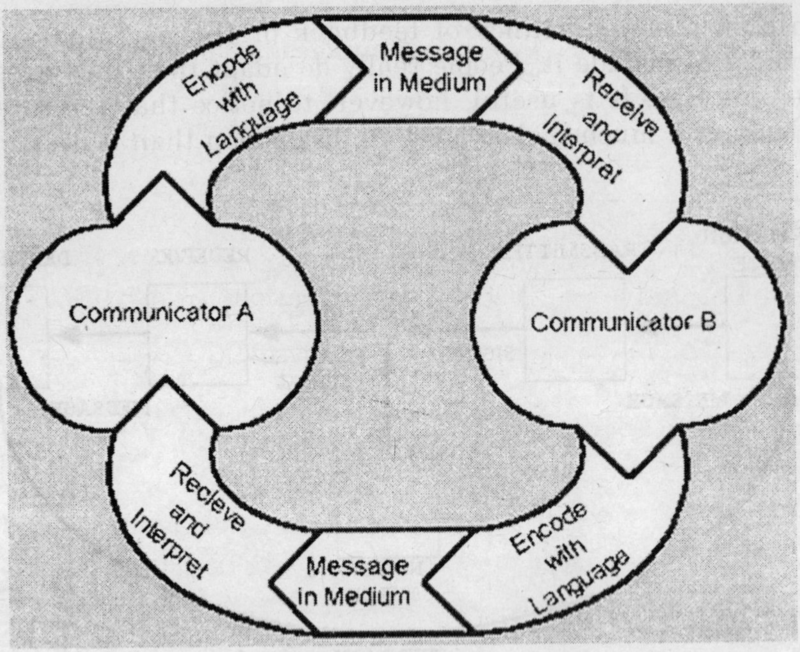

Fig.8.5: A Transactional Model:

"Mass personal" media of the Internet through this implied symmetry into even greater relief. Most Internet media grant everyone symmetrical creation and consumption interfaces. Anyone with Internet access can create a web site and participate as an equal partner in e-mail, instant messaging, chat rooms, computer conferences, collaborative composition sites, blogs, interactive games, MUDs, MOOs, and other media. It remains, however, that users have very different preferences in their message consumption and creation. Some people are very comfortable creating messages for others online. Others prefer to "lurk"; to freely browse the messages of others without adding anything of their own. Adding comments to a computer conference is rarely more difficult than sending an e-mail, but most Internet discussion groups have many more lurkers (consumers of messages that never post) than they have contributors (people who both create and consume messages). Oddly, the lurkers sometimes feel more integrated with the community than the contributors do.

EXERCISE

Q.1 Explain transactional model of communication.

Q.2 Differentiate between intermediary and interactive model of communication.

Q.3 What is Shannon's model of communication process?

Q.4 What is the advantages of Interactive model of communication?

Q.5 What is the advantages and disadvantages of Shannon's model?

Q.6 Explain the terms:

(a) Source

(b) Transmitter

(c) Receiver

(d) Channel

Q.7 Describe Derivative models of communication.

CHAPTER-9

Communication Process

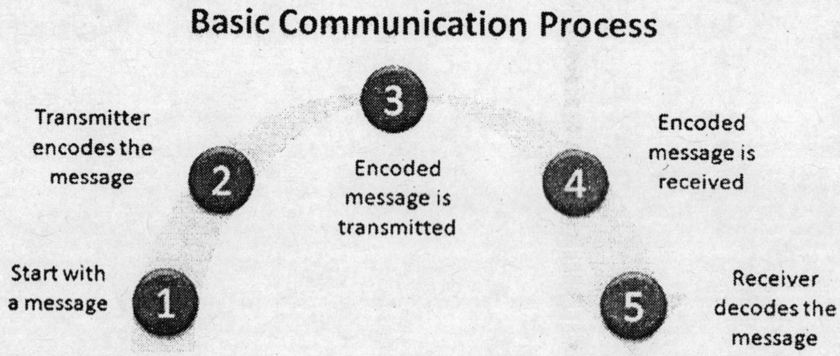

The communication process consists of a message being sent and received. The message may be verbal or non-verbal. The same basic principles apply whether humans, animals, other forms of life, or combinations of these are involved. Your challenge, as an instructor, is to not merely communicate with your students—but to communicate effectively. Effective communication involves a message being sent and received. Added to this however, is the element of feedback to ensure that the message sent was received exactly as intended. This concept may be illustrated using the three-step communications model (fig. 9.1)

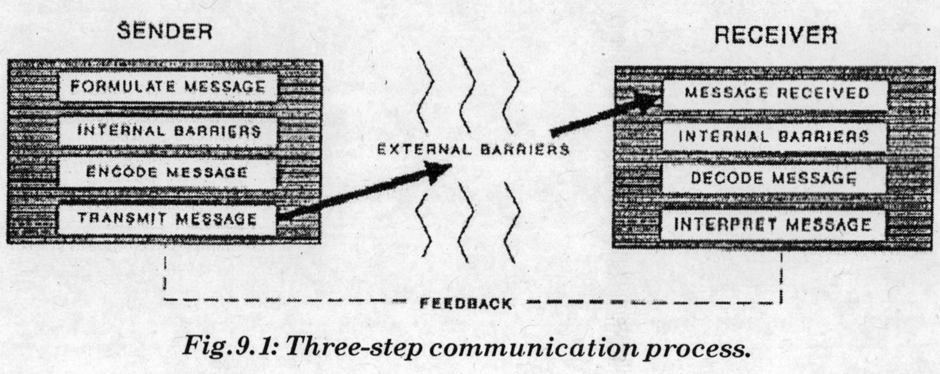

Fig.9.1: Three-step communication process.

Sending the message: There are four elements involved in sending a message. First, as the instructor (sender), you formulate the message you intend to communicate. Next, you consider possible barriers that may affect the message. This includes your experience, the terms you will use, and even your feeling toward the subject or the students. External barriers such as noise must also be considered. Third, you encode the message; that is, you put the message into the words you want to use. Last, you clearly communicate (send) the message.

Receiving the message: There are also four elements involved in receiving a message. The students (receivers) will first hear and/or see the message you sent. Second, the message is affected by external barriers, if any, and the students' own internal barriers. Possible internal barriers may include the students experience level, their understanding of the terms used, their attitude toward the material, or the way they feel about you. Third, your students decode the message through the use of mental images. For instance, when you say the word circus, the receiver does not "see" the letters that form the word. Instead, a mental image of some sort appears. How many different mental images might arise among your students for this one word alone, clown, a big top, lions, acrobats, and so forth? Fourth, the students interpret the message. Clearly, at this point in the process there is no way for you to determine that all of the students received the message you intended. To determine this, you must get feedback.

Feedback, it may take several forms, provides essential information about your success in communicating the message. To get feedback, have the students respond to oral questions and encourage them to ask questions. The students' non-verbal behaviours also provide important clues as to their understanding of the material. Facial expressions and body movements often indicate when students are unsure about the meaning of your message. You should be careful in accepting a "yes" response when you ask "Do you understand?" Obtain meaningful feedback by asking questions that require the students to provide answers which indicate that they in fact do understand exactly what you intended.

Communication barrier

- Introduction
- Wrong choice of medium
- Physical barrier
- Semantic barrier
- Different comprehension of reality
- Socio-psychological barrier
- Questions for assessment

Communication is complete and perfect when the receiver understands the message in the same sense and spirit as the communicator intends to convey, Here, idea and information reached to and responded by receiver remain unaltered and undistorted. But practically it has been noticed that such perfect and complete communication does not take place because of certain obstacles or other factors known as communication barrier.

"There are a lot of causes of misunderstanding and misinterpretations of message communicated. As the process of communication involves sender, channels and receiver, the problem of communication usually lies with either one or more of them.

Problems/ barrier / breakdowns may arise at any of the following levels:

(a) The sender's level in
  (i) Formulating/ organizing thought, ideas, message
  (ii) Encoding the message
(b) The receiver's level in
  (i) Receiving the message;
  (ii) Decoding the received message;
  (iii) understanding/interpreting the message.

- Transmission level where 'noise' occurs.
- The feedback/reaction level that is a necessary condition of the completion of the process.

Miscommunication can originate at three levels: at the level of the transmitter, of the medium, or of the receiver. In technical parlance, anything that Obstructs free flow of communication is called 'noise'. Or we may refer to it simply as a 'barrier' to communication.

Let us consider the following situations:

1. A salesman has to submit a report on the comparative sales figures of the last five years. If he writes a lengthy paragraph incorporating the information, or talks on the phone, he will fail to communicate anything. He should present the figures in a tabular form, or preferably make a bar diagram, which will make communication an instantaneous process.

Wrong choice of Channel

2. An employee wants to express his regrets to his supervisor over his misconduct. In this case, written explanation alone may prove to be ineffective. Face-to-face communication will probably be the best. Let him speak very little, but let him look remorseful; his supervisor will be satisfied and the whole matter will be amicably settled..

3. A manager wants to compliment an employee for a distinguished performance. Shall he send a peon with a memo? Don't we know how memos are usually resented? The manager should choose a medium that transmits his compliments with a personal touch,

   Each communication must be transmitted through an appropriate medium. An unsuitable medium is one of the biggest barriers to communication

Physical barriers

1. **Noise:** Noise is quite often a barrier to communication. In factories, oral communication is rendered difficult by the loud noise of machines. Electronic noise like blaring often interferes in communication by telephone or loudspeaker system. The word 'noise' is also used to refer to all kinds of physical interference like illegible handwriting, smudged copies of duplicated typescript, poor telephone connections, etc.
2. **Time anti Distance:** Time and distance also act as barrier to the smooth flow of communication. The use of telephone along with computer technology has made communication very fast and has, to a large extent, overcome the space barrier. However, sometimes mechanical breakdowns render these facilities ineffective.

In such cases, the distance between the transmitter and the receiver becomes a mighty barrier. Some factories run in shifts. There is a kind of communication gap between persons working in different shifts. Faulty seating arrangement in the room can also become a barrier to effective communication, for whichever seats the employees may be occupying, they definitely want an eye contact with one another.

Physical barrier are:

- **Noise:** noise in a factory; external disturbance in telecom facilities; poor writing; bad photo-copies; etc.
- **Time and distance:** if telecom and network facilities are not available; people working in different shifts; faulty seating arrangement in the hall; etc,

These barriers need just a little care to overcome.

Semantic barrier

1. **Interpretation of words:** Most of the communication is carried on through words, whether spoken or written. But words are capable of communicating a variety of meanings. It is quite possible that the receiver of it message does not assign the same meaning to a word as the transmitter had intended. This may lead to miscommunication. Murphy and Peck in their book Effective Business Communications mention that in an abridged dictionary, the little word 'run' has 71 meanings as a verb, another 35 as a noun, and 4 more as an

adjective. If this word occurs in a message, the receiver is at liberty to interpret it in any of the 110 senses, but if communication is to be perfect, he must assign to it he same meaning as existed in the sender's mind when he used it.

What is the meaning of the word 'value'?

What do we exactly mean when we say, "Radium is a valuable metal"?

Do we refer to its utility or its price, or both?

Peter little in communication in Business asks us to consider the following six sentences:

(i) What is the value of this ring?

(ii) What is the value of learning about communication?

(iii) I value my good name.

(iv) I got good value for my money.

(v) There is something wrong with the tone values in all his paintings.

There is no need to refer to Economics and economic interpretations to understand that in these six sentences, the word 'value' has a series of meanings, or more accurately, a series of areas of meaning. It is only from the context that we can determine which area of meaning is to be assigned to a particular word. But on account of different social, economic, cultural and educational backgrounds, people interpret even the contexts differently. The result is miscommunication.

2. **Bypassed instructions:** Bypassing is said to have occurred if the sender and the receiver of the message attribute different meanings to the same word or use different words for the same meaning. Murphy and Pack have given a classic example of how bypassed instructions can play havoc with the communication process:

   An office manager handed to a new assistant one letter with the instruction, "Take it to our stockroom and burn it." In the office manager's mind (and in the firm's jargon) the word "burn" meant to make a copy on a company machine which operated by a heat process. As the letter was extremely important, she wanted an extra copy. However, the puzzled new employee, afraid to ask questions, burned the letter with a lighted match and thus destroyed the only existing copy.

3. **Denotations and connotations:** Words have two types of meanings: denotative and connotative.

   The literal meaning of a word is called its denotative meaning. It just informs and names objects without indicating any positive or negative qualities. Words like 'table', 'book', 'accounts', and 'meeting' are denotative.

In contrast, connotative meanings arouse qualitative judgements and personal reactions. 'Honest', 'competent', 'cheap', 'sincere', etc., are connotative words.

Some of these words like 'honest', 'noble', 'sincere" are favorable connotations; others like 'cowardly', 'slow', 'incompetent' have unfavorable connotations. But there also exist a large number of troublesome words that have favorable connotations in certain contexts and unfavorable connotations in others. One such word is 'cheap'. Look at the following two sentences:

They gave us cheap stuff.

At this shop, they sell things cheap.

In the first sentence 'cheap' refers to quality and has an unfavorable connotation, in the second one it refers to prices and is used favorably.

To avoid problems arising out of bypassed instructions and connotative meanings of words, the following factors should be constantly kept in mind:

- We should prefer words which are familiar to the receiver in the interpretation we wish to give them.
- If we want the receiver to give an unfamiliar meaning to a familiar word within the context of our message, we should make it amply clear the first time we use it.
- If we feel that a word being used by us is likely to be unfamiliar to the receiver, we should make its meaning clear the first time we use it.
- Whenever possible, we should choose words with positive rather than negative connotations.

Different comprehension of reality

The reality of an object, an event, or a person is different to different people. Reality is not a fixed concept; it is complex, infinite and continually changing. Besides, each human being has limited sensory perceptions and a unique mental filter. No two persons perceive reality in identical manners. On account of different abstractions, inferences, and evaluations, they comprehend reality in a different way. This may sometimes lead miscommunication.

1. **Abstracting:** Abstracting may be defined as the process of focusing attention on some details and omitting others. In numerous cases, abstracting is both necessary and desirable, for it may save us valuable time, space and money

   But abstracting poses a grave barrier to communication, for details which look pertinent to one reporter may look insignificant or trivial to another. We do not make allowances for these differences, and misunderstandings arise. Very often, we yield to the 'allies' fallacy. We believe that whatever we know or say about an object or event is all that is worth knowing or saying about it. And unfortunately the less we know, the more sure we feel that we know it all. We can overcome this barrier if we constantly keep in mind that an abstract can never be the whole story:

(i) While abstracting, we should try to make our abstract as fairly representative of the whole situation as possible.

(ii) We should realize that others can pick different ideas and facts from the same situation and we should be mentally prepared to consider what they have to say about it.

2. **Slanting:** 'Slanting' is giving a particular bias or slant to the reality. In a way, slanting is similar to allies. In allies, we know only a part and are ignorant of the rest, but we think that we know the whole. In slanting, we are aware of the existence of other aspects, but we deliberately select a few and make them representative of the whole. Unfortunately, the aspects that we select are usually unfavorable. If all man is accustomed to heavy drinking, we dub hi as a drunkard and tend to forget that he might also be a good friend, a loyal employee and a kind-hearted man. If one executive of a firm is held guilty of fraud, we begin to suspect every other executive and the image of the firm is spoiled. The overcome this barrier, we should try to be objective in our observations and assessments and we should try to avoid the mistake of judging the whole by what might be only a fraction of it.

3. **Inferring:** What we directly see, hear, feel, taste, smell or can immediately verify and confirm constitutes a fact. But the statements that go beyond facts and the conclusions based on facts are called inferences. When we drop a letter in the post box, we assume that it will be picked up and carried to the post office, when we say that the Kalka Mail will leave on time. If rains fail, we can infer that prices will go up. Some of these inferences are fairly reliable.

While drawing inferences, we should carefully distinguish between facts and assumptions and make sure that our inferences are based on verifiable facts.

Socio-psychological barriers

1. **Altitudes and opinion:** Personal, attitude and opinion often act as barriers to effective communication If information agrees with our opinions and attitudes, we tend to receive it comfortably. It fits comfortably in the filter of our mind. But if information disagrees with our views or tends to run contrary to our accepted beliefs; we do not react favorably. If a change in the policy of an organization proves advantageous to an employee/ he welcome it as good; if it affects him adversely, he rejects it as the whim of the Director.

2. **Emotions:** Emotional states of mind play an important role in the act of communication. If the sender is perplexed, worried, excited, afraid, nervous, his thinking will be blurred and he will not be able to organize his message properly. The state of his mind is sure to be reflected in his message. It is a matter of common observation that people caught in a moment of fury succeed

only in violent gesticulation. If they try to speak, they falter and keep on repeating the same words. In the same way, the emotions of the receiver also affect the communication process. If he is angry, he will not take the message in proper light.

3. **Closed mind:** A person with a closed mind is very difficult to communicate with. He is a man with deeply ingrained prejudices. And he is not prepared to reconsider his opinions. He is the kind of man who will 'say, "Look, my mind is made up. I know what I know. And I do not want to know anything else. So just don't bother me." You approach such a man with a new proposal to improve his business and he will immediately retort, "Look here gentleman, do you presume that you know my business better than I know? I have been in this line for the last twenty years. What can you teach me?" Such a person is not open to conviction and persuasion. And in all likelihood, he has not learnt anything in the twenty years he has been in business.

   If closed-minded people can be encouraged to state their reasons for rejecting a message or a proposal, they may reveal deep-rooted prejudices/' opinions and emotions. Perhaps, one can make an attempt to counteract those prejudices, opinions, etc. But if they react only with anger and give a sharp rebuff to anyone who tries to argue with them, they preclude all possibility of communication.

4. **Status-consciousness:** Status consciousness exists in every organization and is one of the major barriers to effective communication. Subordinates are afraid of communicating upward any unpleasant information. They are either too conscious of their inferior status or too afraid of being snubbed. Status-conscious superiors think that consulting their juniors would be compromising their dignity.

   Status-consciousness proves to be a very serious barrier to face-to-face communication. The subordinate feels jittery and nervous, fidgets about where he is standing, falters in his speech and fails in communicating what exactly he wanted to say. The officer, on the other hand, reveals impatience and starts giving comments or advice before he has fully heard his subordinate. Consequently, there is a total failure of communication; the subordinate returns to his seat dissatisfied and simmering inside, while the officer resumes his work with the feeling that his employees have no consideration for the value of his time and keep on pestering him for nothing.

5. **The source of communication:** If the receiver is suspicious about or prejudice against the source of communication, there is likely to be a barrier to communication. People often tend to react more according to their attitude to the source of facts than to the facts themselves. Think of an executive in

the habit of finding fault with his employees. If once in a while he begins with a compliment, the employees immediately become suspicious and start attributing motives to the compliment. If a statement emanates from the grapevine, the manager will not give credence to it, but the same statement coming from a trusted supervisor will immediately be believed.

6. **Inattentiveness:** People often become inattentive while receiving a message in particular, if the message contains a new-idea. The human mind usually resists-change, for change makes things uncertain. It also threatens security and stability. So the moment a new idea is presented to them, they unconsciously become inattentive.
7. **Faulty transmission:** A message is never communicated from one person to another in its entirety. This is true in particular of oral messages. If a decision has been taken hy the Board of Directors, it must be in the form of a lengthy resolution. This resolution cannot be passed on to the factory workers in the same form. It has to be 'translated' in simple language so that they may easily understand it. But translation can never be perfect. In the process of interpretation, simplification and translation, a part of the message gets lost or distorted. A scientific study of the communication process has revealed that successive transmissions of the same message are decreasingly accurate. In oral communications, something in the order of 30 per cent of the information is lost in each transmission.
8. **Poor retention:** Poor retention of communication also acts as a barrier. Studies show that employees retain only about 50 per cent of the information communicated to them. The rest is lost. Thus if information is communicated through three or four stages, very little reaches the destination, and of that very little also only a fraction is likely to be retained.

   Poor retention may lead to imperfect responses, which may further hamper the communication process.
9. **Unsolicited communication:** Unsolicited communication has to face stronger barriers than solicited communication. If I seek advice, it should be presumed that I will listen to it. But if a sales letter comes to me unsolicited, it is not very sure that I will pay much attention to it.

Socio-psychological barriers

- **Attitudes and opinions:** We react favorably or are hostile according as the information is to our personal advantage or not.
- **Emotions:** We can neither transmit thing correctly 'if our mind is agitated.
- **Closed mind:** We hold our opinion so rigidly that we just refuse to listen.
- **Status-consciousness:** We are over-conscious of our lower or higher rank and do not express ourselves candidly.

- **The source of communication:** We react according to the trust we repose in the source from which the communication originates.
- **Inattentiveness:** Unconsciously we become inattentive if the communication contains a new idea and our mind refuses to respond to it.
- **Faulty transmission:** Part of the message is lost in transmission.
- **Poor retention:** 'Oral messages in particular are lost due to poor human retention.
- **Unsolicited communication:** We are unresponsive if the communication is unsolicited.

CASE STUDY

A French executive frequently had to give presentations to senior executives in his company.

Problem: His English was excellent, but because of his heavy French accent, he was often misunderstood. He used gestures that made him look wildly excited and distracted listeners from what he was saying. Furthermore, his presentations had many busy tables, and his messages were confusing and unclear resulting in twelve to eighteen bullet points per slide instead of the six to eight that people can absorb. He relied on his PowerPoint to do the presentation for him instead of speaking freely and persuasively.

Solution: We video taped several of his presentations. When he saw and heard himself on film, he realized he had to contain his movements while he was presenting, and, he also realized that he had quite a heavy accent. By analyzing the materials and vocabulary which he used in presentations and in informal speeches, he was able to practice the correct intonation of his most frequently used phrases. He also worked on keeping his hands to his sides and keeping movements to a minimum. And, he remembered to smile. We identified the main messages he wanted to focus on and organized his presentations so that he had plenty of time to practice before his talk was due.

Results: He was very satisfied with what he and learned and how much he had changed his speech in quite a short time. It gave him more self confidence and he was able to concentrate more on what he said than worry about how he sounded. He learned to outline his speeches and presentations before writing them in PowerPoint and now, he not only sounded clearer and more organized, but it also took him a lot less time to prepare. He learned to use PPT as a tool and not as a substitute. Currently we are working on his giving speeches without the help of his computer, he talks with just a few overheads that show the tables to which he refers and he speaks freely the rest of the time.

EXERCISE

Q.1 What are the different barriers in communication.

Q.2 Describe semantic barrier.

Q.3 Describe Shanno's model of communication.

Q.4 What are the main physical barriers of communication?

Q.5 Explain Interactive model of communication.

Q.6 Explain Derivative models of communication.

Q.7 Give some of the socio psychological barriers of communication.

Q.8 Explain clearly the process of communication. (May-2008)

Ans.: Process of communication

Communication is a two-way process in which there is an exchange of ideas or thoughts linking the sender and receiver towards a mutually accepted direction or goal consisting of 7 elements which are as under:

1. Sender: The process of communication begins with a sender, the person who has an idea and desires to exchange it.
2. Encoding: The sender puts his/her ideas or facts into words, symbols, pictures or gestures that the receiver can understand.
3. Message: A message refers to what is being communicated. It may be verbal or non-verbal.
4. Channel: Channel is the medium through which message is transmitted to the sender. Channel may be in oral or written forms.
5. Receiver: It is any person who notices and attaches some meaning to a message.
6. Decoding: The receiver translates the words and symbols used in the message into ideas and interpret it to attain its meaning.
7. Feedback: Ultimately receiver reacts or responds to the communication sent by the sender. It could be based on clear interpretation of the symbols sent or misunderstanding or misinterpretation of the symbols sent.

CHAPTER-10

Corporate Communication

Corporate communication is the communication issued by a corporate / organization / body / institute to all its public. "Publics" here can be both internal (employees, stakeholders, i.e. share and stock holders) and external (agencies, channel partners, media, government, industry bodies and institutes, educational institutes and general public).

An organization needs to talk the same message to all of its stakeholders, in order to transmit coherence, credibility and ethic. If one of these points is broken, the whole community can make this organization disappear. The Corporate Communication area will help this organization to build its message, combining its vision, mission and values and will also support the organization by communicating its message, activities and practices to all of its stakeholders.

Therefore the term Corporate Communication can be defined as the set of activities involved in managing and orchestrating all internal and external communications aimed at creating favorable starting points with stakeholders on whom the company depends. Corporate communication consists of the dissemination of information by a variety of specialists and generalists in an organization, with the common goal of enhancing the organization's ability to retain its license to operate.

Note that it is corporate communication—without a final "s". Tired of being called on to fix the company switchboard, recommend an answering machine or meet a computer salesman, I long ago adopted this form as being more accurate and left communications to the telecommunications specialists. It's a small point but another attempt to bring clarity out of confusion.

Corporate communication serves as the link between an organization and its publics.

Organizations can strategically communicate to their audiences through public relations and advertising. This may involve an employee newsletter or video, crisis management with the news media, special events planning, building product value and communicating with stockholders, clients or donors.

Basic forms: Formal and informal Communication

Communication can be formal and informal. However, formal communication does not mean written communication. For example, a verbal reprimand from a manager to a subordinate is a form of formal communication, whereas a written joke passed around the office is a form of informal communication.

The purposes of informal communication are:-

1. To satisfy personal needs;
2. To prevent boredom;
3. To provide information relevant to the job that is not provided by formal channels.

FORMAL COMMUNICATION

- Communication takes place through the formal channels of the organization structure along the lines of authority established by the management.
- Such communications are generally in writing and may take any of the forms; policy; manuals: procedures and rule books; memoranda; official meetings; reports, etc.

Advantages & Disadvantages of Formal Communication:

The **advantages** of formal communication are:

- They help in the fixation of responsibility and
- Maintaining of the authority relationship in an organization.

The **disadvantages** of formal communication are:

- Generally time consuming, cumbersome and
- Leads to a good deal of distortion at times.

INFORMAL COMMUNICATION

- Communication arising out of al those channels of communication that fall outside the formal channels is known as informal communication.
- Built around the social relationships of members of the organization.
- Informal communication does not flow lines of authority as is the case of formal communication.
- It arises due to the personal needs of the members of organization.
- At times, in informal communication, it is difficult to fix responsibility about accuracy of information. Such communication is usually oral and may be covered even by simple glance, gesture or smile or silence.

Grapevine Communication (Informal Business Communication)

The term grapevine communication is often used interchangeably with the term informal communication. The term originated in the 1860s during the American Civil War. It was used as a term that described the telegraph lines that were strung through the trees in a manner that resembled grapevines. It also came to mean informal communication that was not very effective because the telegraph system was not a reliable source of communication at the time. Almost a century later, it was discovered that the path of grapevine communication does resemble a cluster of grapes.

It has been shown that informal communication or grapevine communication occurs when formal communication is not sufficient. Research and studies have concluded that informal communication occurs either when insufficient of ambiguous information is transmitted through formal communication. Some organizational theorists feel that some informal or grapevine communication is needed in organizational life.

The way grapevine communication works is one person, Person 1, sends a message to Person 2 and Person 3. Then, Person 2 tells Person 4 and Person 5. And Person 3 tells Person 6. Not all participants within the grapevine send messages. Some participants are just receivers. Liaisons within an organization usually help facilitate grapevine communication. The use of this type of communication is common among managers as well as subdivision employees.

The types of rumors that are spread through grapevine communication can be classified into two groups, spontaneous and premeditated. Spontaneous rumors are spread when people are stressed or in an untrustworthy environment. Premeditated rumors spread within highly competitive environments. These two groups can be broken down into four classifications: wish fulfillment, anxiety, wedge drivers, and home stretchers. These types of rumors can also be spread through other types of informal network structures such as the single strand chain, the cluster chain, the probability chain, and the gossip chain.

The formal network, made up of memos, reports, staff meetings, department meetings, conferences, company newsletters and official notices is highly documented and as such has very little chance for change. However, nearly all of the information within the grapevine is undocumented and is thereby open to change and interpretation as it moves through the network. It often travels faster than formal channels. The grapevine is very useful in supplementing formal channels. It provides people with an outlet for their imaginations and apprehensions as well. It also helps satisfy a natural desire to know what is really going on. The primary objective of this article is to develop a conceptual model to be tested later. The article defines tile term rumor/grapevine, discusses reasons for grapevine, explore show accurate is grapevine, type of grapevine, how grapevine is spread, role of various participants and how to manage the grapevine. Dealing effectively with the grapevine is a challenge that will always be a part of a manager's job. Those who are able to understand the power of the grapevine will be better prepared to utilize it to provide stability and credibility in the work environment that is needed in order to achieve organizational goals.

Grapevine is American as mom and apple pie. Grapevine is an integral part of the American political and social system as shown by, e.g., Iran-contra episode, defrocking of Jim Bakker, Boesky scandal and the demise of presidential hopeful Gary Hart, etc. It is a vital part of democracy, Franklin Roosevelt kept an ear close to it, and Richard Nixon and his plumbers tried to stifle it. What is it' Ignored by some, feared by some and used by many. It is the grapevine. That nebulous, all-seeing, all-knowing network of "truth" If you want to know the real story or the "kernel of truth" tune into the grapevine.

The dictionary gives us a definition for the grapevine which says it is "the informal transmission of information, *gossip* or rumor from person to person" The grapevine is the informal and unsanctioned information network within every organization. "The network helps employees make sense of the world around them and consequently provides a release from emotional stress and all informal information is undocumented." (One of the leading authors on the subject) discovered in his study that organizational Grapevine is an expression of healthy human motivation to communicate: "In fact, if employees are so uninterested in their work that they do not engage in shoptalk about it, they are probably maladjusted." Of all the things that the grapevine has been called, it is foremost—a communications network.

Since it is unstructured and not under complete control of management, it moves through the organization in every direction. "It moves upwards, downward, and diagonally, within and without chains of command, between workers and managers, and even with and without a company."

The term grapevine can be traced to Civil War days when vine like telegraph wires were strung from tree to tree across battlefields and used by Army Intelligence. The messages that came over these lines were often so confusing or inaccurate that soon any rumor was said to come from the grapevine. Usually, grapevines flow around water coolers, down hallways, through lunch rooms, and wherever people get together in groups. The lines of communication seem to be haphazard and easily disrupted as the telegraph wires were, however, they transmit information rapidly and in many cases faster and with a stronger impact than the formal system allows.

Location of the Grapevine

Since the grapevine arises from social interactions, it is as fickle, dynamic, and varied as people are. It is the expression of their natural motivation to communicate.

It is the exercise of their freedom of speech and is a natural, normal activity. The grapevine starts early in the morning in the car pools. once everyone has arrived at work, grapevine activity takes place nearly all day long down hallways, around corners, in meetings, and especially by the coffee machine. The peak time of the days are breaks and lunch hour during which management has little or no control over the topics of conversation. In the late afternoon the work day has finished but the grapevine has not. After a short time interval, some employees meet again. They are on company softball teams, golf leagues, and bowling teams. The grapevine at that time goes into full swing again and remains active with one final activity peak at a local bar. The following day, the cycle is repeated. It is the wide range of locations where the grapevine takes place in combination with the fact that grapevine participants come from informal social groups within the organization which points out it's difference from formal management communication. Structured management uses verbal messages to communicate through the chain of command, while grapevine communication jumps from one department to another and from any level of management to another. It moves up, down, horizontally, vertically and diagonally all within a short span of time. The grapevine, as communication, can be compared to the organizations formal information network.

Formal vs. Informal Channels of Communication

Every organization has a formal communication system. This formal system provides information regarding the organization to the employees through different media. The formal network, made up of memos, reports, staff-meetings, department meetings, conferences, company newsletters, official notices, is highly documented and as such has very little chance for change. However, nearly all of the information within the grapevine is undocumented and is thereby open to change and interpretation as it moves through the network. "The informal organization is less permanent and less stable (than the formal organization) because its leaders and patterns of action change readily." This occurs because of the dependency of the network on personalities, whereas the formal network is set up through structured policies nondependent on individuals.

Keith Davis did a classic study of the grapevine in 1953. This was followed by an extension of the research by Harold Sutton and Lyman Porter in 1968. Keith Davis stated "the grapevine is a natural part of a company's total communication system...it is a significant force within the work group, helping to build teamwork motivate people, and create corporate identity." The grapevine is the informal passing of information through the organization. It does not necessarily follow the formal structure of the organization and can bypass individuals without restraint. It can be more direct and faster than the formal channels of information since the information is not being screened or controlled. It often travels faster than formal channels. Interestingly, it has been found that the grapevine is equally active both in management and among the workers. The grapevine exists in organizations for many reasons. Grapevine communication can carry useful information through the organization with amazing speed. The grapevine is very useful in supplementing formal channels. It provides people with an outlet for their imaginations and apprehensions as well. It also helps satisfy a natural desire to know what is really going on and gives employees a sense of belonging. As an early warning system, gossip allows people to think through in advance what they will do if the rumors become the awful truth. Subordinates may get an idea of what the boss is wrestling with and may have some suggestions which may help the situation.

The grapevine is flexible and personal and can spread information faster than the formal communication channels. The grapevine is also capable of penetrating even the tightest security because it cuts across organizational lines and deals directly with people in the know. Bosses who chose not to pay attention to the grapevine have 50% less credible information than those who do. Khandwalla states that it exists because of excessive structuring of formal work flows and the excessive channeling of information flows.[9] It is fed by personal apprehension, wish fulfillment, retaliation, and gossip. Surprisingly, most researchers have found that most grapevine information is either true or has within it a kernel of truth.

Reasons for Grapevine Communications

Grapevines exist in all organizations in varying degrees. Gordon Allport describes two conditions as controlling activeness of the grapevine; importance of the subject to the speaker and listener, and the ambiguousness of the facts. He relates the two with the following formula:

$$R = IA$$

Where:

R is the intensity of the rumor

I is the importance of the rumor to the persons communicating, and

A is the ambiguity of the facts associated with the rumor.

This formula, according to all port, means that the amount of rumor in circulation will vary with the importance of the subject to the individuals concerned times the ambiguity of the evidence pertaining to the topic at issue. The relation between importance and ambiguity is not additive but multiplicative, for if either importance or ambiguity is zero, there is no rumor. This formula is supported by Donald B. Simmons who states it slightly differently. He states "rumors originate, grow, and spread along the grapevine in direct proportion to their importance to workers and the lack of news on a subject from official channels."

How Accurate is the Grapevine?

Allport and Postman's research indicated that "most rumors start as a report of an actual episode-that is to say, with someone's perceptual experience of an event which he deems of sufficient interest and importance to communicate to others.

Once this central theme, the actual episode, has been accepted there is a tendency to distort subsequent news or events in order to make them consistent with the central theme. However, Keith Davis reports from his research "that in normal business situations between 75 percent and 95 percent of grapevine information is correct."

In general people tend to think the grapevine is less accurate than it is because its errors tend to be more dramatic and consequently are more impressed on one's memory than its day-to-day routine accuracy.

In a normal work situation, upwards of 80% of the information that comes over the grapevine is accurate. While the day-to-day accuracy may be good, people believe the grapevine is less accurate because the times it is wrong are more dramatic. A communication may be 90% correct in details but that last 10% is often the most important part of the message. Messages from the grapevine are often lacking in all the details so that the message is subject to misinterpretation; while the grapevine generally carries the truth it seldom carries the whole truth.

An interesting note about the informal communications network is that an estimated 80% of grapevine information is oriented toward the individual while 20% concerns the company.

Allport and Postman discuss, in their book, the changes that occur as a rumor passes along the grapevine. The central theme may be resistant to change, however crucial details necessary for understanding the true situation keep being deleted. (They call the process "leveling. ") At the same time the most dramatic details keep being exaggerated each time the rumor is repeated. (This they refer to as "sharpening.") So as the rumor moves along it begins to appear as some sort of shrinking missile as it keeps getting shorter and more pointed in flight

This may sound very simple, however we should remember that " the grapevine is fast-paced and generally moves, free of organizational restraints, by word of mouth."

Factors Affecting Grapevine's operation

Several additional factors affect the operation of the grapevine. First, in wartime, the conditions for rumor are optimal. Military events are of the greatest importance. Second, the greater the homogeneity of the organization, the better the grapevine will operate. Third, rumors prosper best where formal communication is poor. They thrive in an environment where employees are not kept informed about anything that my be important to them. Fourth, they perform best in informal social contacts but can operate as effectively as a sideline to official meetings. In a poorly managed organization they can chip away at morale and fuel anxiety, conflict, and misunderstanding. Fifth, people start and spread rumors to enhance their status, fill gaps in social conversations, and avoid suspense over suspected events. This activity increases during times of stress, uncertainty, and in the absence of news.

Frederick Koenig, a sociologist who studies rumors, believes that people listen to and pass a rumor because it satisfies some need. This is why the nature of people involved is important. Different people have different needs and rumors...

a) May circulate because they are interesting or a source of diversion. The valve can be the content of the message or the state of the group.
b) Can pull together events and fill in the gaps to make sense and provide explanations for what is going on.
c) Can validate and support a point of view.
d) Reconcile one's psychological state with what one sees as actually going on. (Studies show people who are high in anxiety are more frequent participants in the rumor process and groups in stressful situations have more rumor activity.)
e) Are a means of getting attention..
f) Are a way of manipulating situations, the idea of some person or group deliberately starting a rumor to serve selfish ends is frequently suggested.

Types of Rumors

We will now take a look at the types of rumors that travel the grapevine. But, before we look at the types we should be aware of the two overall classifications that apply to all rumors. These are explained by Roy Rowan. The two classifications are: Spontaneous rumors and Premeditated rumors.

Spontaneous rumors appear during periods of stress and thrive in an atmosphere of anxiety, mistrust, repression of utter chaos. These rumor die as soon as they become irrelevant.

On the other hand, premeditated rumors, as might be expected, are often planted for Machiavellian purposes, particularly in highly competitive environments.

Rumors that fall into both classifications have been witnessed travelling along most companies' grapevines. However, the spontaneous rumor is seen most often as facts are pieced together to explain an occurrence.

Research has determined that much of what the grapevine carries is rumors. These rumors can be concerning any practice or policy of the company or about any person in the company. Rumors can be divided into four (4) categories. The first category is that of the "wish fulfillment or pipe dreams:"

Pipe dreams or wish fulfillment—these express the wishes and hopes of those who circulate rumors and these are the most positive and they help to stimulate the creativity of others. Often solutions to work problems are a result of employees verbally expressing desire for changes. These improvements sometimes result in increased efficiency for certain departments within the organization. Even though the tone is positive they still represent employee concerns.

The second category is that of the "anxiety," or "bogie," rumor:

The Bogie rumor—comes from employees' fears and anxieties causing general uneasiness among employees such as during budget crunch. In this case, employees will verbally express their fears to others. These rumors are sometimes damaging, such as a rumor about possible lay-offs, and need a formal rebuttal from management.

The majority of rumors fall into the category of the "aggressive rumors, " or "wedge drivers," or "Motel Six" types of rumors:

Wedge Drivers—divide groups and destroy loyalties. They are motivated by aggression or even hatred. They are divisive and very negative rumors. They tend to be demeaning to a company or individual and can cause damage to the reputation of others. A wedge driver rumor may be someone at x Company saying that v Company serves worms in their hamburgers; or in another context, a school-age child telling friends that another child has AIDS, or some other tale, like "Louise, the office manager, was seen the other day alone with that young new accountant. They were in a car together leaving Motel Six." or one may spread the word that "Mary got the promotion because she is sleeping with the boss." Women are more likely to be attacked with the sexual gossip.

Home-Stretchers—These are anticipatory rumors. These rumors occur after employees have been waiting a long time for an announcement. There may be just one final thing necessary to complete the puzzle and this in effect enhances the ambiguity of the situation.

Now that we have discussed why the grapevine exists, the accuracy of the information on the grapevine and the types of rumors that exist, we will look at how the message is spread and those who participate.

How is the word spread?

Within the organization communication chains exist. The chain used by formal communication may be very rigid, following the chain of command or authority. However, the chain used by the grapevine tends to be very flexible. Four different chains/structures appear to dominate the grapevine network according to Keith Davis are:

1. The Single Strand Chain This is a simple concept to follow, A tells B, who tells C, who tells D and so on. Each person passes the information on to the next person. The longer the strand the more distortion and filtering affects

the information being passed until the last person in the chain may find the information unrecognizable from the original message. Most inaccuracies occur in this chain.

2. The Gossip Chain: In this illustration A simply tells everyone with whom they come in contact. This pattern is considered to be somewhat slow in moving the information.
3. The Probability Chain: In this case A makes random contact with say F and C and passes on the information. They in turn randomly contact others in accordance with laws of probability. Some hear the information and some don't. In this structure, there is no definite pattern of communication. Information is randomly passed along to anyone willing to listen. They type of person who communicates in this manner might be a very outgoing and talkative type of individual.
4. The Cluster Chain: Here A tells contacts, B and F, who may work with A. They may tell two or three other persons with whom they usually have close contact. Most predominant pattern is the cluster pattern. Selectivity is the basis for this pattern. In any organization, individuals will generally feel more comfortable with some fellow employees than with others and therefore only relay information to those in their informal social groups. This flow pattern results in information missing some individuals completely.

Roles of the Participants

In addition to identifying certain structured patterns, research has also given us some other facts and descriptions, It has been discovered that only 10% of all the individuals in an organization are highly active participants in the grapevine. The types of individuals relative to rumors, have been identified. The three are bridgers, baggers, and bearers. Most employees fall into one of the three (3) basic categories as they relate to the grapevine.

1. Bridgers or Key Communicators - Bridgers or key communicators receive and pass information to others. These people are the ones primarily responsible for the success of the grapevine. Bridgers—are the passers-along; the liaisons of rumors, also called KC's, as explained by Sutton. "Key Communicator" is the term that is given to this type of individual who is responsible for initially sending information into various networks.
2. Baggers or Dead Enders - Baggers hear rumors but do not pass them along or fail to tell others. They are called "dead-enders." They receive information but do not pass it on or only pass it on to one or maybe two other dead-enders.
3. Beaners or Isolates - Beaners, or isolates, are not privy to any information, do not hear the information and thus cannot pass along, a rumor. They tend

to be outside the grapevine. They neither hear nor pass along the information.

Each type of individual can easily be identified in the communication mains previously illustrated. It should also be noted that people are more active on the grapevine when their friends and colleagues are actively involved.

After all that has been said about the grapevine the next questions that arise are: What should the company managers do about the grapevine? Is it good or bad? Should the managers participate? How do we manage the grapevine?

Management's Response to the Grapevine

The key thing to remember is that the grapevine exists, William A. Delaney reminds us of this when he says the "grapevine exists, always has and always will, and you can't stop it." So managers should accept the fact and decide how they can use it to their own benefit.

Vanessa Arnold contends that "Managers interested in creating effective organizational communication will use information from the grapevine to improve communication throughout the firm."

The real value of the grapevine should be in revealing to management those issues that generate from the grass roots. As Donald Thompson said "its usefulness is seldom acknowledged, its voice often muffled, its insights ignored."

Should Managers Participate?

In many cases lower and middle managers are already active participants. They hold strategic positions in the communication channel because they filter and block two-way communication between higher management and operating employees.

Managers basically have three options when it comes to their participation in the grapevine:

1. Ignore the grapevine, be no part of it. This is difficult in most organizations, but can be accomplished. They do their job and let it operate unnoticed around them. In effect they become an "isolate. "
2. Participate only when it serves their purpose. In this case they may seek out the grapevine and tap it to learn what is being said concerning a specific situation or issue.
3. Become an active and full-time participant.

Coping or Managing the Grapevine

Since the grapevine cannot be held responsible for errors and is somewhat of an unknown, managers sometimes succumb to the wish that it will go away; but we have learned from experience and research that "homicide" will not work with the grapevine. It cannot be abolished, rubbed out, hidden under a basket, chopped down, tied up, or stopped. If we suppress it in one place it will pop up in another. If we cut off one of its sources, it merely moves to another one...It is as hard to kill as the mythical glass snake, that, when struck, broke itself into fragments and grew a new snake out of each piece. In a sense, the grapevine is a human birthright, because whenever people congregate into groups, the grapevine is sure to develop. It may use smoke signals, jungle tom-tome, taps on a prison wall, ordinary conversation, or some other method, but it will always be there. Organizations cannot "fire" the grapevine because they did not hire it. It is simply there.

Positive Aspects

Even though management does not always view it favorable, the grapevine has several positive aspects. One major advantage of the grapevine is that it is a release mechanism for stress. Bottled-up feelings have been proven to have negative side effects for individuals and the grapevine helps to ease this type of situation. We know individuals like and need to talk about their work. It's and important part of one's life, The grapevine provides a soapbox for individuals to talk about this important facet of their lives. In talking about work, the grapevine gives employees the opportunity to convert official company policies into their own language or jargon. In doing this, individuals are better able to understand the policies and are better able to cope with their work environment. This open communication also enables employees to have empathy for those who are occurring stress outside of the work place. As stronger personal bonds occur among workers, a greater spirit of team work exists within the organization.

Because of the speedy transfer of information, the grapevine enables individuals to prepare for and think through management's goal changes and goal adjustment in advance of any formal statements. This increases the contributions of employees. The grapevine also helps employees to remain efficient by quickly spreading the news of disciplinary action. If tardiness is a problem and one person is given a day off without pay, will management be able to remind everyone immediately of company policy? Probably not. Will a memo from the Personnel Department reach everyone that same day? That isn't likely to happen either. However, will the grapevine make sure everyone's at work on time the next day? oh, yes!

Additionally, the grapevine is a good indicator of health, morale, trends, and productivity. The grapevine reveals issues and problems being discussed by the employees; the effect of policies and procedures upon which the employees can be measured. Managers should have some means of tapping into the grapevine. The grapevine is also a means of communication which a manager can use for efficiency. Via this method, desired information can be circulated quickly to a large group of subordinates. Control of the grapevine is an understated responsibility of the manager. While all the information passing through is not initiated by management, management is ultimately responsible for its accuracy.

Management Options

Internal rumors are generally managed differently than external rumors if for no other reason than management of a company has more control over internal formal communication than over information sent out to the external environment.

Since grapevine activity increases during times of uncertainty, management must provide information through the formal system of communication about key issues and events that affect employees. Management should supply employees with a steady flow of accurate, timely information; in this way, the potential damage caused by the grapevine can be minimized. Any attempt to soften or distort a rumor to make things look good is not a good way to deal with the rumor. The longer a rumor circulates the more difficult it is to control. Facts should be released quickly. The grapevine can be controlled with prompt, clear, and accurate information on the issues important to the employees. Full facts must be presented. Formal communication lines must be kept open and the process as short as possible. Direct memos, large group announcements, and intercom systems should be used. If employees perceive management is giving them the facts, they will be less anxious and less emotional when rumors are heard.

Although the preferred management option is prevention, this never works 100% of the time. In other words, there will be negative rumors and if one wants to manage them, one ought to be prepared. So when prevention doesn't work, and it won't, what can one do? Two methods are suggested. First, a four-step method, and second, a disciplined three-phase management program, Generally, in the four-step method, four steps are suggested:

1. Seek to keep employees informed about what is going on. A formal company newsletter always seems to help.
2. Heed rumors. Listen to what is being said that is 80% true. What other information source is so highly credible?
3. Act promptly. Rumors are more difficult to correct over time because they "harden"—the details become consistent and the information becomes publicly accepted,
4. Conduct a training program for employees on the nature of rumors.

For the wedge drivers and the bogies, although prevention is the preferred method of management. This will fail sometimes. When it does, a rather disciplined, three-phase management program can be used incorporating both the tapping of the grapevine and the active management of the formal communications channels.

Phase I. Active gathering of information regarding the rumor

1. Ascertain extent of rumor's circulation. Can you be at a distant friend's retirement party and hear a bad rumor about your company. ..or...Do you

merely receive a roomful of laughs when you walk into your service club's monthly meeting?

2. Collect facts. Recalling that 80% of rumors are true, corporate leaders at Upjohn discovered that rumors about massive kickbacks to foreign governments by its international division were true. It is thus wise to look, or at least know, where one is leaping.
3. Assess sources of uncertainty and anxiety. Rumors are a product of someone's anxiety. That rumors in response to uncertainty, it seems logical to determine what the uncertainty is all about.

Having done all of Phase I, make a decision as to whether the rumor will die on its own merits or whether it will continue to the detriment of the company. If it is decided that the rumor will continue, proceed to the second phase.

Phase II. Prepare for a public response through the development of an information dissemination plan.

1. Prepare a formal response, With external rumors, the company does not control the channels of communication. This is left to journalists, reporter, and announcers. Preparing a formal response that provides an opportunity to access the various mass media is absolutely crucial to even getting in the front door, front page, or six o'clock news.
2. Begin work on preparing an information dissemination plan. This plan is to directly counter-attack the public rumor, now generally to the point of public fact, in a direct and intentional way.

Before proceeding to Phase III, review again whether the rumor will die of its own weight, silliness, or irrelevancy, or really is becoming a nuclear cloud over your company, It is to the point of not being able to go away on its own, you may decide to implement the plan developed in Phase III.

Phase III. Implement the plan.

Besides the above two methods, i.e. a) four-step method, and b) a disciplined three phase management program, the authors feel that tapping of the grapevine is also important. First of all, management can try to identify and make use of key communicators. Management can leak out important information to key communicators or bridgers who actively transmit information. By participating, management can monitor what is happening in the organization and discover the reactions of its employees.

The grapevine can be used to see how a new idea will be received. If feedback through the grapevine indicated an unfavorable reaction, management can reconsider the idea or alter it to lessen employee resistance. If the new idea is incorporated, management will be forewarned of problems and can be prepared with new programs to help overcome anxiety and misperceptions. In short, as an early warning system, rumors allow management to think through in advance. John Kotter, a Harvard Business School professor and author of "Power and Influence," "gives an example of a manager he knows who uses the grapevine to give new ideas a "trial-run" before spending a great deal of time and money. "He knows who in the office has the longest tongue," explains Kotter. He than casually mentions this new idea to the employee and waits for the word to spread. In no time, responses find their way back to his secretary, who gives him a full report. Feedback is very important, and if it is positive, he goes ahead with the new plan. If the feedback is negative, it's back to the drawing board to rethink the idea and pinpoint the problem areas. The simple, cheap way to check an idea can be invaluable to a manager.

Some organizations create a rumor hotline or rumor control office. When an employee hears a rumor he can call the rumor office to check it out. By providing this service, bad rumors can be replaced with good rumors. Good rumors, such as "I asked about that and was told it wasn't so," move just as quickly through the grapevine as bad ones, and can increase morale, help build teamwork, and increase motivation. Dealing effectively with the grapevine is a challenge that will always be a part of a manager's job. Those who are able to understand the power of the grapevine will be better prepared to utilize it to provide stability and credibility in the work environment that is needed in order to achieve organizational goals.

Grapevine is an informal channel of business communication. It is called so because it stretches throughout the organization in all directions irrespective of the authority levels. Man as we know is a social animal. Despite existence of formal channels in an organization, the informal channels tend to develop when he interacts with other people in organization. It exists more at lower levels of organization.

Grapevine generally develops due to various reasons. One of them is that when an organization is facing recession, the employees sense uncertainty. Also, at times employees do not have self-confidence due to which they form unions. Sometimes the managers show preferential treatment and favor some employees giving a segregated feeling to other employees. Thus, when employees sense a need to exchange their views, they go for grapevine network as they cannot use the formal channel of communication in that case. Generally during breaks in cafeteria, the subordinates talk about their superior's attitude and behavior and exchange views with their peers. They discuss rumors about promotion and transfer of other employees. Thus, grapevine spreads like fire and it is not easy to trace the cause of such communication at times.

Examples of Grapevine Network of Communication

1. Suppose the profit amount of a company is known. Rumor is spread that this much profit is there and on that basis bonus is declared.
2. CEO may be in relation to the Production Manager. They may have friendly relations with each other.

Pros and Cons of Grapevine Communication

Advantages of Grapevine Communication

1. Grapevine channels carry information rapidly. As soon as an employee gets to know some confidential information, he becomes inquisitive and passes the details then to his closest friend who in turn passes it to other. Thus, it spreads hastily.
2. The managers get to know the reactions of their subordinates on their policies. Thus, the feedback obtained is quick compared to formal channel of communication.
3. The grapevine creates a sense of unity among the employees who share and discuss their views with each other. Thus, grapevine helps in developing group cohesiveness.
4. The grapevine serves as an emotional supportive value.
5. The grapevine is a supplement in those cases where formal communication does not work.

Disadvantages of Grapevine Communication

1. The grapevine carries partial information at times as it is more based on rumours. Thus, it does not clearly depict the complete state of affairs.
2. The grapevine is not trustworthy always as it does not follows official path of communication and is spread more by gossips and unconfirmed report.
3. The productivity of employees may be hampered as they spend more time talking rather than working.
4. The grapevine leads to making hostility against the executives.
5. The grapevine may hamper the goodwill of the organization as it may carry false negative information about the high level people of the organization.

A smart manager should take care of all the disadvantages of the grapevine and try to minimize them. At the same time, he should make best possible use of advantages of grapevine.

Non Verbal Communication

Definition "nonverbal communication involves those nonverbal stimuli in a communication setting that are generated by both the source [speaker] and his or her use of the environment and that have potential message value for the source or receiver [listener]. Basically it is sending and receiving messages in a variety of ways without the use of verbal codes (words). It is both intentional and unintentional. Most speakers / listeners are not conscious of this. It includes — but is not limited to:

- Touch

- glance
- eye contact (gaze)
- volume
- vocal nuance
- proximity
- gestures
- Facial expression? Pause (silence).
- intonation
- dress
- posture
- smell
- word choice and syntax
- sounds (paralanguage)

Broadly speaking, there are two basic categories of non-verbal language:

- Nonverbal messages produced by the body;
- Nonverbal messages produced by the broad setting (time, space, silence)

Why is non-verbal communication important?

Basically, it is one of the key aspects of communication (and especially important in a high-context culture). It has multiple functions:

- Used to **repeat** the verbal message (e.g. point in a direction while stating directions).
- Often used to **accent** a verbal message. (e.g. verbal tone indicates the actual meaning of the specific words).
- Often **complement** the verbal message but also may contradict. e.g.: a nod reinforces a positive message (among Americans); a "wink" may contradict a stated positive message.
- **Regulate** interactions (non-verbal cues covey when the other person should speak or not speak).
- May **substitute** for the verbal message (especially if it is blocked by noise, interruption, etc) — i.e. gestures (finger to lips to indicate need for quiet), facial expressions (i.e. a nod instead of a yes).

Note the implications of the proverb: "Actions speak louder than words." In essence, this underscores the importance of non-verbal communication. Non-verbal communication is especially significant in intercultural situations. Probably non-verbal differences account for typical difficulties in communicating.

Cultural Differences in Non-verbal Communication

1. **General Appearance and Dress:** All cultures are concerned for how they look and make judgments based on looks and dress. Americans, for instance, appear almost obsessed with dress and personal attractiveness. Consider differing cultural standards on what is attractive in dress and on what constitutes modesty.
2. **Body Movement:** We send information on attitude toward person (facing or leaning towards another), emotional statue (tapping fingers, jiggling coins), and desire to control the environment (moving towards or away from a person).

More than 700,000 possible motions we can make — so impossible to categorize them all! But just need to be aware the body movement and position is a key ingredient in sending messages.

Posture Consider the following actions and note cultural differences:

- o Bowing (not done, criticized, or affected in US; shows rank in Japan)
- o Slouching (rude in most Northern European areas)
- o Hands in pocket (disrespectful in Turkey)
- o Sitting with legs crossed (offensive in Ghana, Turkey)
- o Showing soles of feet. (Offensive in Thailand, Saudi Arabia)
- o Even in US, there is a gender difference on acceptable posture?

3. **Gestures:** Impossible to catalog all but need to recognize:
   1. Incredible possibility and variety and
   2. That an acceptable in one's own culture may be offensive in another. In addition, amount of gesturing varies from culture to culture. Some cultures are animated; other restrained. Restrained cultures often feel animated cultures lack manners and overall restraint. Animated cultures often feel restrained cultures lack emotion or interest.

Even simple things like using hands to point and count differ.

Pointing: US with index finger; Germany with little finger; Japanese with entire hand (in fact most Asians consider pointing with index finger to be rude)

Counting: Thumb = 1 in Germany, 5 in Japan, middle finger for 1 in Indonesia.

4. **Facial Expressions:** While some say that facial expressions are identical, meaning attached to them differs. Majority opinion is that these do have similar meanings world-wide with respect to smiling, crying, or showing anger, sorrow, or disgust. However, the intensity varies from culture to culture. Note the following:

- Many Asian cultures suppress facial expression as much as possible.
- Many Mediterranean (Latino / Arabic) cultures exaggerate grief or sadness while most American men hide grief or sorrow

- Some see "animated" expressions as a sign of a lack of control.
- Too much smiling is viewed in as a sign of shallowness.
- Women smile more than men.

Eye Contact and Gaze, In USA, eye contact indicates: degree of attention or interest, influences attitude change or persuasion, regulates interaction, communicates emotion, defines power and status, and has a central role in managing impressions of others.

- Western cultures — see direct eye to eye contact as positive (advise children to look a person in the eyes). But within USA, African-Americans use more eye contact when talking and less when listening with reverse true for Anglo Americans. This is a possible cause for some sense of unease between races in US. A prolonged gaze is often seen as a sign of sexual interest.
- Arabic cultures make prolonged eye-contact. — believe it shows interest and helps them understand truthfulness of the other person. (A person who doesn't reciprocate is seen as untrustworthy)
- Japan, Africa, Latin American, Caribbean — avoid eye contact to show respect.

Touch:

Question: Why do we touch, where do we touch, and what meanings do we assign when someone else touches us?

Illustration: An African-American male goes into a convenience store recently taken over by new Korean immigrants. He gives a $20 bill for his purchase to Mrs. Cho who is cashier and waits for his change. He is upset when his change is put down on the counter in front of him.

What is the problem? Traditional Korean (and many other Asian countries) doesn't touch strangers especially between members of the opposite sex. But the African-American sees this as another example of discrimination (not touching him because he is black).

Basic answer: Touch is culturally determined! But each culture has a clear concept of what parts of the body one may not touch. Basic message of touch is to affect or control— protect, support, disapprove (i.e. hug, kiss, hit, kick).

- USA — handshake is common (even for strangers), hugs, kisses for those of opposite gender or of family (usually) on an increasingly more intimate basis. Note differences between African-Americans and Anglos in USA. Most African Americans touch on greeting but are annoyed if touched on the head (good boy, good girl overtones).
- Islamic and Hindu: typically don't touch with the left hand. To do so is a social insult. Left hand is for toilet functions. Mannerly in India to break your bread only with your right hand (sometimes difficult for non-Indians)

- Islamic cultures generally don't approve of any touching between genders (even hand shakes). But consider such touching (including hand holding, hugs) between same-sex to be appropriate.
- Many Asians don't touch the head (Head houses the soul and a touch puts it in jeopardy).

Basic patterns: Cultures (English, German, Scandinavian, Chinese, and Japanese) with high emotional restraint concepts have little public touch; those which encourage emotion (Latino, Middle-East, Jewish) accept frequent touches.

Smell

- USA — fear of offensive natural smells (billion dollar industry to mask objectionable odors with what is perceived to be pleasant) — again connected with "attractiveness" concept.
- Many other cultures consider natural body odors as normal (Arabic).
- Asian cultures (Filipino, Malay, Indonesian, Thai, and Indian) stress frequent bathing — and often criticize USA of not bathing often enough!

Paralanguage

- Vocal characterizers (laugh, cry, yell, moan, whine, belch, and yawn). These send different messages in different cultures (Japan — giggling indicates embarrassment; India – belch indicates satisfaction)
- Vocal qualifiers (volume, pitch, rhythm, tempo, and tone). Loudness indicates strength in Arabic cultures and softness indicates weakness; indicates confidence and authority to the Germans,; indicates impoliteness to the Thais; indicates loss of control to the Japanese. (Generally, one learns not to "shout" in Asia for nearly any reason!). Gender based as well: women tend to speak higher and more softly than men.
- Vocal segregates (un-huh, shh, uh, ooh, mmmh, humm, eh, mah, lah). Segregates indicate formality, acceptance, assent, uncertainty.

IMPORTANCE OF COMMUNICATION IN BUSINESS

Communication is essential for life in general but in business settings, it is critical. Communication is more than just a matter of speaking and hearing, especially within a business setting. Good communication, on the other hand, means that your message will be sent and that the people or organizations understand the message in its entirety. Further, they are much more likely to respond in a positive manner if the message was communicated effectively. A poorly communicated message will likely be resulted in an unfavorable response.

Communication is one of the basic functions of management in any organization and its importance can hardly be overemphasized. It is a process of transmitting information, ideas, thoughts, opinions and plans between various parts of an organization.

You cannot have human relations without communication. However, good and effective communication is required not only for good human relations but also for good and successful business. You can use software's like business writing software for writing effective business communication, which is required at various levels and for various aspects in an organization such as :-

Importance of communication for manager and employee relations:

Effective communication of information and decision is an essential component for management-employee relations. The manager cannot get the work done from employees unless they are communicated effectively of what he wants to be done? He should also be sure of some basic facts such as how to communicate and what results can be expected from that communication. Most of management problems arise because of lack of effective communication. Chances of misunderstanding and misrepresentation can be minimized with proper communication system.

For motivation and employee morale:

Communication is also a basic tool for motivation, which can improve morale of the employees in an organization. Inappropriate or faulty communication among employees or between manager and his subordinates is the major cause of conflict and low morale at work. Manager should clarify to employees about what is to be done, how well they doing and what are can be done for better performance to improve their motivation. He can prepare a written statement, clearly outlining the relationship between company objectives and personal objectives and integrating the interest of the two.

For increase productivity:

With effective communication, you can maintain a good human relation in the organization and by encouraging ideas or suggestions from employees or workers and implementing them whenever possible, you can also increase production at low cost.

CASE STUDY

A Korean engineer had problems being understood and expressing himself about his job in English.

Problem : It took his team too much of an effort to work with him when they had software problems. His fellow employees tried to skip meeting with him because they felt they lost too much time every time they had to meet with him. Therefore, he was out of the picture very often and missed key pieces of information.

Solution: Intense language/ESL lessons several times a week, with a strong emphasis on foreign accent reduction.

Results: He had much more confidence speaking and the others could understand him better. However, it is something he will have to continue to work on. When he had to stop the training after 2 months, he was by no means where he could have been with more training and practice. However, we were contacted to work with him again.

EXERCISE

Q.1 What do you understand by corporate communication?

Q.2 Describe formal and informal communication.

Q.3 What do you understand by Grapewine communication. Give some examples.

Q.4 Explain some of the cultural differences in non verbal communication.

Q.5 What are the main disadvantages of grapewine communication?

Q.6 What is the importance of non verbal communication?

Q.7 What is the advantage of informal communication?

Q.8 What is the disadvantage of informal communication?

Q.9 What are the advantages and disadvantages of formal communication?

Q.10 What is the importance of communication in business environment?

Q.: Explain clearly the meaning of the term "Grapevine' as applicable to communication.

(May-2008)

Ans.: Grapevine as applicable to communication: Communication may be oral or written for direct contact. It may be informal also. The "Grapevine" is one of the recognized channels of informal communication. According to human psychology, a person likes to form and move in groups. They interact on serious and non- serious issues and they spread it fast whether the information is correct or not. This process is known as rumour mill. The larger the organization, the more active is the rumor mill. The phenomenon of grapevine is based on generally three factors, namely

1. Formation of favored group
2. Lack of self confidence and,
3. Feeling of uncertainty due to lack of directions. Four kinds of the grapevine chains have been identified and they are:

(a) Single Strand Chain, which is the least accurate in passing on the information or message.

(b) Gossip Chain, which is often used when information or a message regarding 'not-on- job' nature is being conveyed.

(c) Probability Chain is used when information is somewhat interesting but not really significant.

(d) Cluster Chain, which acts as liaison and spreads information with the greatest speed.

Q.: Explain the factors which are responsible for the growing importance of communication of an organization.

(June-2009)

Ans.: The importance of communication in the industrial organization has increased immensely in these days. The following factors are responsible for the growing importance of communication:

1. Growth in the size and multiple location of organizations: Most of the organization are growing larger and larger in size. The people are working in the country and abroad, of these organizations. Keeping in touch, sending directions across and getting feedback is possible only when communication lines are kept working effectively.
2. Growth of trade unions: Over the last so many decades, trade unions have been growing strong. No management can be successful without taking the trade unions into confidence. Effective communication will create relationship between the management and the workers.
3. Growing importance of human relations: Workers in an organization are not like machines. They have their own hopes and aspirations. Management has to recognize them and should work with the sprit of integration so that human relations may be maintained. This may only be achieved though effective communication.
4. Public relations: Every organization has a social responsibility towards customers, government, suppliers and the public at large. Communication is the only way an organization can project a positive image of itself.
5. Advances in behavioral sciences: Modern management is deeply influenced by exciting discoveries made in behavioral sciences like psychology, sociology, transactional analysis etc. All of them throw light on suitable aspects of human nature and help in developing a positive attitude towards life and building up meaningful relationship. This is possible only through communication.
6. Technological advancement: The world is changing very fast, owing to scientific and technological advancements. These advancements deeply affect not only the methods of work but also the compositions of groups. In such a situation, proper communication between superiors and subordinates becomes very necessary.

Q.: What are the merits and demerits of grape-vine form of Communication?

(November-2009)

Ans.: Merits of the grapevine form of communication:

(a) Speedy transmission: The greatest merit of this phenomenon is that it transmits information very speedily. A rumor spreads like wild fire. The very moment a worker comes to know that something is 'top secret' or 'confidential' he/she tries to look into it or have some idea of it and pass it on to others. Thus it spreads within minutes. Managers have been known to distribute information through planned 'leaks' or carefully used 'just between you and me' remarks as part of grapevine communication

(b) Feedback value: It is primarily through the grapevine that the managers or top bosses of an organization get the feedback regarding their policies, decisions, memos etc. The feedback reaches them much faster through the informal channel than through the formal channel.

(a) Support to other channels: The grapevine or informal channel functions as a supplementary or parallel channel of communication. The formal channels not only take more time but also impose certain constraints on the process of communication. So, whatever is deemed to be unsuitable for the formal channels can be successfully transmitted through the grapevine form of communication?

(b) Psychological satisfaction: The grapevine gives immense psychological satisfaction to the workers and strengthens their solidarity. It draws them nearer to each other and thus keeps the organization intact as a social entity.

Demerits:

(a) It is less credible. It cannot always be taken seriously.

(b) It does not always carry the complete information.

(c) It often distorts the picture or often misinforms.

CHAPTER-11

Letter Writing

Letters are very important and effective means of communication. Since the time man learned to write he has been using this art to express himself and convey his thoughts and feelings. It is an art that can be mastered by observation and practice. The main skill to cultivate is to make the recipient of the letter trust your words. The language of the letter reflects your personality, so choose words with care. The language of the letter should be simple and expressive with accuracy and appropriateness. There are two main types of letters namely:

FORMAL LETTERS

- Layout of a formal letter
- Formal letter writing rules
- Content of a formal letter
- Abbreviations used in letter writing
- Outline for a covering letter
- Outline for a letter of enquiry

Layout of a Formal Letter

The example letter below shows you a general layout for a formal letter.

33–Rajpur Road
Dehradun-248001
Uttarakhand
22 December 2007

The Headmaster
ST. Thomas
Ghanta Ghar

Dear Sir or Madam

I should be grateful if you would send me information about the regulations for admission to the Hall School of Design. Could you also tell me whether the school arranges acccomodation for students?

Yours Faithfully

Allan P

A.K. Pratap

Example of formal letter

Rules for Writing Formal Letters in English

In English there are a number of conventions that should be used when writing a formal or business letter. Furthermore, you try to write as simply and as clearly as possible, and not to make the letter longer than necessary. Remember not to use informal language like contractions.

Addresses:

1. **Your Address:** The return address should be written in the top right-hand corner of the letter.
2. **The Address of the person you are writing to** the inside address should be written on the left, starting below your address.

Date:

Different people put the date on different sides of the page. You can write this on the right or the left on the line after the address you are writing to. Write the month as a word.

Salutation or greeting:

1. **Dear Sir or Madam:** If you do not know the name of the person you are writing to, use this. It is always advisable to try to find out a name.
2. **Dear Mr Jenkins:** If you know the name, use the title (Mr, Mrs, Miss or Ms, Dr, etc.) and the surname only. If you are writing to a woman and do not know if she uses Mrs or Miss, you can use Ms, which is for married and single women.

Ending a letter:

1. **Yours faithfully:** if you do not know the name of the person, end the letter this way.
2. **Yours sincerely:** If you know the name of the person, end the letter this way.
3. **Your signature:** Sign your name, then print it underneath the signature. If you think the person you are writing to might not know whether you are male of female, put you title in brackets after your name.

CONTENT OF A FORMAL LETTER

First paragraph

The first paragraph should be short and state the purpose of the letter- to make an enquiry, complain, request something, etc.

The paragraph or paragraphs in the middle of the letter should contain the relevant information behind the writing of the letter. Most letters in English are not very long, so keep the information to the essentials and concentrate on organising it in a clear and logical manner rather than expanding too much.

Last Paragraph

The last paragraph of a formal letter should state what action you expect the recipient to take- to refund, send you information, etc.

Abbreviations Used in Letter Writing

The following abbreviations are widely used in letters:

- **asap** = as soon as possible
- **cc** = carbon copy (when you send a copy of a letter to more than one person, you use this abbreviation to let them know)
- **enc.** = enclosure (when you include other papers with your letter)
- **pp** = per procurationem (A Latin phrase meaning that you are signing the letter on somebody else's behalf; if they are not there to sign it themselves, etc)
- **ps** = postscript (when you want to add something after you've finished and signed it)
- **pto** *(informal)* = please turn over (to make sure that the other person knows the letter continues on the other side of the page)
- **RSVP** = please reply

Outline: A Covering Letter

A covering letter is the one that accompanies your CV when you are applying for a job. Here is a fairly conventional plan for the layout of the paragraphs.

Opening Paragraph

Briefly identify yourself and the position you are applying for. Add how you found out about the vacancy.

Paragraph 2

Give the reasons why you are interested in working for the company and why you wish to be considered for that particular post. State your relevant qualifications and experience, as well as your personal qualities that make you a suitable candidate.

Paragraph 3

Inform them that you have enclosed your current CV and add any further information that you think could help your case.

Closing Paragraph

Give your availability for interview, thank them for their consideration, restate your interest and close the letter.

Outline: A Letter of Enquiry

A letter of enquiry is when you are approaching a company speculatively, that is you are making an approach without their having advertised or announced a vacancy.

Opening Paragraph

Introduce yourself briefly and give your reason for writing. Let them know of the kind of position you are seeking, why you are interested and how you heard about them.

Paragraph 2

Show why their company in particular interests you, mention your qualifications and experience along with any further details that might make them interested in seeing you.

Paragraph 3

Refer to your enclosed CV and draw their attention to any particularly important points you would like them to focus on in it.

Closing Paragraph

Thank them, explain your availability for interview and restate your enthusiasm for their company and desire to be considered for posts that might as yet be unavailable.

Informal Letters

All official, business letters are formal letters. Whereas all letters to relatives and friends are informal letters. But there are certain rules to be followed in each case.

5th November 2010

Dear Nilansh,

Oh, how I missed being with you during the holidays this year! Everything in Dehradun is so different from Delhi that I don't know if I'll ever get used to living here. I'm so glad that my father's job at the Govt. sector will only last until June. Then we will come home, and you and I can spend the summer on the beach. (I hope you'll spend your holiday in Goa, as usual.)

I've already made some very nice friends, but don't worry - no one could ever replace you as my best friend! After school, I sometimes go to my friend Fiona's house. She enjoys listening to the same music and watching the same clips that you and I like. In fact, Fiona and I have tickets for Bon Jovi's concert next month. I wish you were coming with us!

Life is very different here. Would you believe that we have to wear a uniform to go to school? It's awful! A blue skirt and blazer, a white blouse and a ridiculous checked tie, not to mention a pair of horrible, long, white socks. Besides, there is nothing to do in the evening. All the shops close by 4.30 p. m. and pubs are only open till 11 p. m.

That's all for now; I must start my homework for my English class tomorrow. The teacher wants us to write an informal letter to a friend and I don't even know where to begin! Please write soon and tell me all the news. I miss you.

Love,

Rahul

Business letter/correspondence

In our day to-day life we exchange our ideas, thoughts and other information with our friends, relatives and other people. Sometimes we directly talk to them and sometimes we also write letters to them. In letters we express our feelings in a few words, we may ask for any information or we may write about a complaint in connection with our problems. Similarly businessmen also exchange ideas, information by writing letters. They communicate business information to customers, suppliers and others and at the same time receive a variety of letters from them. In this lesson let us know about different types of letters used in the process of business transactions.

Objectives

After studying this lesson, you will able to state the meaning of Business Correspondence; explain the importance of Business Correspondence; describe the essential qualities of a good business letter; identify the various parts of a business letter; and recognize the different types of letters used in business.

Meaning of Business Correspondence

Communication through exchange of letters is known as correspondence. We communicate our feelings, thoughts, etc. to our friends and relatives through letters that may be called personal correspondence. A Businessman also writes and receives letters in his day to-day transactions, which may be called business correspondence.

Business correspondence or business letter is a written communication between two parties. Businessmen may write letters to supplier of goods and also receive letters from the suppliers. Customers may write letters to businessmen seeking information about availability of goods, price, quality, sample, etc. or place order for purchase of goods. Thus, business letters may be defined as a media or means through which views are expressed and ideas or information is communicated in writing in the process of business activities.

Importance of Business Correspondence

Now-a-days business operations are not restricted to any locality, state or nation. Today production takes place in one area but consumption takes place everywhere. Since the businessmen as well as customers live in far off places they don't have sufficient time to contact each other personally. Thus, there arises the need for writing letters. In the past the situation was not so. Business letters were not essential in olden days. But now the importance of letters has increased because of vast expansion of business, increase in demand as well as supply of goods. Let us learn about the importance of business letters.

Help in maintaining proper relationship.

Now-a-days business activities are not confined to any one area or locality. The businessmen as well as customers are scattered throughout the country. Thus, there is a need to maintain proper relationship among them by using appropriate means of communication. Here business letters play an important role. The customers can write letters to the businessman seeking information about products and businessmen also supply various information to customers. This helps them to carry on business on national and international basis.

Inexpensive and convenient mode

Though there are other modes of communication like telephone, telex, fax, etc. but business information can be provided and obtained economically and conveniently through letters.

Create and maintain goodwill

Sometimes business letters are written to create and enhance goodwill. Businessmen at times send letters to enquire about complaints and suggestions of their customers. They also send letters to inform the customers about the availability of a new product, clearance sale, etc. All this results in cordial relation with the customers, which enhances the goodwill of the business.

Serves as evidence

We cannot expect a trader to memories all facts and figures in a conversation that normally takes place among businessmen. Through letters, he can keep a record of all facts. Thus, letters can serve as evidence in case of dispute between two parties.

Help in expansion of business

Business requires information regarding competing products, prevailing prices, promotion, market activities, etc. If the trader has to run from place to place to get information, he will end up doing nothing. It will simply result in loss of time. But through business letters, he can make all enquiries about the products and the markets. He can also receive orders from different countries and, thus enhance sales.

I. Fill in the blanks with suitable words.

(i) Business letters serve as a/an .... in case of dispute in business transactions.

(ii) It is .... for the businessmen to remember all facts without correspondence.

(iii) Business letters build .... for a businessman.

(iv) Business letters are written to .... information.

(v) Business letter is the most .... mode of communication.

II. Given below are certain statements. Write 'T' against true statements and 'F' against false statements.

(i) Letter is a form of written communication.

(ii) Through business letter personal contact can be maintained between buyer and seller.

(iii) Business letters lead to decline the goodwill of the firm.

(iv) Letter is a convenient and economic mode of communication.

(v) Business letters do not help in removing misunderstanding between buyer and seller.

Essential Qualities of a Good Business Letter

A letter should serve the purpose for which it is written. If a businessman writes a letter to the supplier for purchase of goods, the letter should contain all the relevant information relating to the product, mode of payment, packaging, transportation of goods, etc. clearly and specifically. Otherwise, there will be confusion that may cause delay in getting the goods. Again the quality of paper used in the letter, its size, colour etc. also need special attention, because it creats a positive impression in the mind of the receiver. We may classify the qualities of a good business letter as:

(a) Inner Qualities; and

(b) Outer Qualities

(a) Inner Qualities: The inner qualities of a good business letter refer to the quality of language, its presentation, etc. These facilitate quick processing of the request and that leads to prompt action. Let us discuss the various inner qualities of a good business letter.

(i) **Simplicity**: Simple and easy language should be used for writing business letters. Difficult words should be strictly avoided, as one cannot expect the reader to refer to the dictionary every time while reading letter.

(ii) **Clarity:** The language should be clear, so that the receiver will understand the message immediately, easily and correctly. Ambiguous language creates confusion. The letter will serve the purpose if the receiver understands it in the same manner in which it is intended by the sender.

(iii) **Accuracy:** The statements written in the letter should be accurate to, the best of the sender's knowledge. Accuracy demands that there are no errors in the usage of language - in grammar, spellings, punctuations, etc. An accurate letter is always appreciated.

(iv) **Completeness**: A complete letter is one that provides all necessary information to the users. For example, while sending an order we should mention the desirable features of the goods, i.e., their quality, shape, colour, design, quantity, date of delivery, mode of transportation, etc.

(v) **Relevance:** The letter should contain only essential information. Irrelevant information should not be mentioned while sending any business correspondence.

(vi) **Courtesy:** Courtesy wins the heart of the reader. In business letters, courtesy can be shown or expressed by using words like please, thank you, etc.

(vii) **Neatness**: A neat letter is always impressive. A letter either handwritten or typed should be neat and attractive in appearance. Overwriting and cuttings should be avoided.

(b) Outer Qualities: The outer qualities of a good business letter refer to the appearance of the letter. It includes the quality of paper used, colour of the paper, size of the paper etc. Good quality paper gives a favorable impression in the mind of the reader. It also helps in documenting the letters properly. Let us discuss the various outer qualities of a good business letter.

(i) **Quality of paper**: The paper used should be in accordance with the economic status of the firm. Now-a-days the cost of the paper is very high. Therefore, good paper should be used for original copy and ordinary paper may be used for duplicate copy.

(ii) **Colour of the Paper**: It is better to use different colours for different types of letters, so that the receiver will identify the letters quickly and prompt action can be taken.

(iii) **Size of the paper**: Standard size paper (A4) should be used while writing business letters. The size of the paper should be in accordance with the envelopes available in the market.

(iv) **Folding of letter:** The letter should be folded properly and uniformly. Care should be taken to give minimum folds to the letter so that it will fit the size of the envelope. If window envelope is used then folding should be done in such a way that the address of the receiver is clearly visible through the transparent part of the envelope.

(v) **Envelope**: The size and quality of the envelope also need special attention. The size of the letter should fit the size of the letters. The business firms use different types of envelopes, i.e. ordinary envelope, window envelope, laminated envelope, etc. In window envelope there is no need to write the address of the receiver separately on the envelope. It is clearly visible through the transparent part on the face of the envelope, which may be called as window. In laminated envelope a thin plastic sheet or cloth is pasted on the inner side that gives extra protection to letters from being damaged during transit.

IN TEXT QUESTIONS

I. Fill in the blanks with suitable words.

(i) Apart from ordinary envelopes, we may also use ________ or ________ envelopes for sending business letters.

(ii) To make a letter courteous, words like ________ and ________ should be used.

(iii) Business letter should contain only ________ information.

(iv) Accuracy demands no error in the usage of ________.

(v) Business letters should be always neat and ________ in appearance.

II. Match the following.

a) The receiver understands the messagein the same way as intended by the sender

(ii) Relevance

(b) There should be no errors in the usage of language in business letter.

(ii) Courtesy

(c) Relevant information should beprovided in business letter

(iii) Accuracy

(d) Words of anger should not be used in any business letters.

(iv) Clarity

PARTS OF A BUSINESS LETTER

We have discussed above the qualities of a good business letter. The quality will be maintained if we give proper attention to each and every part of the letter. Let us now learn about the different parts of a business letter.

The essential parts of a business letter are as follows:

Different parts of a business letter-

1. Heading	2. Date
3. Reference	4. inside address
5. Subject	6. Salutation
7. Body of the letter	8. Complimentary close
9. Signature	10. Enclosures
11. Copy Circulation	12. Post Script

The essential parts of a business letter are as follows:

1. **Heading:** The heading of a business letter usually contains the name and postal address of the business, E-mail address, Web-site address, Telephone Number, Fax Number, Trade Mark or logo of the business (if any)
2. **Date**: The date is normally written on the right hand side corner after the heading as the day, month and years. Some examples are 28th Feb., 2003 or Feb. 28, 2003.
3. **Reference**: It indicates letter number and the department from where the letter is being sent and the year. It helps in future reference. This reference number is given on the left hand corner after the heading. For example, we can write reference number as AB/FADept./2003/27.
4. **Inside address**: This includes the name and full address of the person or the firm to whom the letter is to be sent. This is written on the left hand side of the sheet below the reference number. Letters should be addressed to the responsible head e.g. the Secretary, the Principal, the Chairman, the Manager, etc. Example:

M/S Virtual
Nanda Complex
Delhi, v2, Complex
Delhi 000011

The Chief Manager,
State Bank of India
Icfai University Campus
Dehradun
Dehradun-248001

5. **Subject:** It is a statement in brief, that indicates the matter to which the letter relates.

   It attracts the attention of the receiver immediately and helps him to know quickly

   what the letter is about. For example,

   Subject: Your order No. C317/8 dated 12th March 2003.

   Subject: Enquiry about Samsung television

   Subject: Fire Insurance policy
6. **Salutation** - This is placed below the inside address. It is usually followed by a comma (,). Various forms of salutation are:

Sir/Madam:	For official and formal correspondence
Dear Sir/Madam:	For addressing an individual
Dear Sirs/Dear Madam:	For addressing a firm or company.
7. **Body of the letter**: This comes after salutation. This is the main part of the letter and it contains the actual message of the sender. It is divided into three parts.

(a) Opening part: It is the introductory part of the letter. In this part, attention of the reader should be drawn to the previous correspondence, if any. For example- with reference to your letter no. 326 dated. 12th March 2003, I would like to draw your attention towards the new brand of television.

(b) Main part: This part usually contains the subject matter of the letter. It should be precise and written in clear words.

(c) Concluding Part: It contains a statement the of sender's intentions, hopes or expectations concerning the next step to be taken. Further, the sender should always look forward to getting a positive response. At the end, terms like Thanking you,

With regards, With warm regards may be used.

8. Complimentary close: It is merely a polite way of ending a letter. It must be in accordance with the salutation. For example:

Salutation	Complementary close
(a) Dear Sir/Dear Madam	Yours faithfully
(b) Dear Mr. Rahul	Yours sincerely
(c) My Dear Akash	Yours very sincerely
	Express very informal relations.)

1. Signature: It is written in ink, immediately below the complimentary close. As far as possible, the signature should be legible. The name of the writer should be typed immediately below the signature. The designation is given below the typed name. Where no letterhead is in use, the name of the company too could be included below the designation of the writer.

For example:

Yours faithfully
For M/S A.K.Brothers
(Signature)
Puneet
Partner

10. Enclosures: This is required when some documents like cheque, draft, bills, receipts, lists, invoices etc. are attached with the letter. These enclosures are listed one by one in serial numbers. For example :

Encl:

(i) The list of goods received

(ii) A cheque for Rs. One Thousand dt. Feb. 27,2003 (Cheque No........) towards payment for goods supplied.

11. Copy circulation: This is required when copies of the letter are also sent to persons apart of the addressee. It is denoted as C.C. For example,

C.C.

(i) The Chairman, Electric Supply Corporation

(ii) The Director, Electric Supply Corporation

(iii) The Secretary, Electric Supply Corporation

12. Post script: This is required when the writer wants to add something, which is not included in the body of the letter.

It is expressed as P.S. For example,

P.S. - In our offer, we provide two years warranty.

Format of a Business Letter

Tel. Name of the firm E-mail: Fax.

Postal Address Website:

Ref. Dated:

To

Name and address of the person to whom letter is sent

Subject

Salutation,

Opening part ______________________________

Main part ______________________________

Concluding part ______________________________

Complementary close

Signature

(name)

Designation

Enclosures

CC-

PS-

IN-TEXT QUESTIONS

Fill in the blanks

(a) The complementary close must be in accordance with the ________.

(b) Below the signature and name of the writer, his ____ is also written.

(c) In the main part of the body of the letter _____ is written.

(d) Dear Sir is the form of __________.

(e) The body of the letter is usually divided into ______ part(s).

After having some idea about the various qualities and different parts of a good business letter let us know about the different types of letter used in business correspondence.

TYPE OF BUSINESS LETTERS

Business letters are written for the fulfillment of several purposes. The purpose may be to enquire about a product to know its price and quality, availability, etc. This purpose is served if you write a letter of enquiry to the supplier. After receiving your letter the supplier may send you details about the product as per your query. If satisfied, you may give order for supply of goods as per your requirement. After receiving the items, if you find that the product is defective or damaged, you may lodge a complaint. These are the few instances in which business correspondence takes place. Let us learn the details about some important business letters.

BUSINESS ENQUIRY LETTER

Sometimes prospective buyers want to know the details of the goods which they want to buy, like quality, quantity, price, mode of delivery and payment, etc. They may also ask for a sample. The letter written to sellers with one or more of the above purposes is known as enquiry letter.

Specimen of Business Enquiry Letter

Tel. 2531566
Fax. 23244155
Ref. PR/F/2002/27

M/s NIS
6/d, C.G mkt.

E-mail: jobsindoon@gmail.com
Website: http://www.NIS.com
Dated: July 27,2002

M/s Virtual
Chauhan Market
Dehradun
Uttaranchal – 248001

Subject: Enquiry about the prices of fans

Dear Sir,

We are dealing in retail trade of electrical appliances. We would be interested in selling your product, NIS through our retail showroom.

Could you, therefore, send us your quotations and let us know the terms and conditions of payment.

Thanking you,

Yours faithfully,
For M/s NIS
(Puneet Gupta)
Partner.

Points to be kept in mind while writing letters of enquiry-

- Letters of enquiry should clearly state the information required, which may be asking for a price list or a sample.
- Write specifically about the design, size, quantity, quality, etc. about the product or service in which the buyer is interested.
- The period or the date, till which information is required, may also be mentioned.

QUOTATION LETTER

After receiving the letter of enquiry from a prospective buyer, the sellers supply the relevant information by writing a letter that is called quotation letter. These letters are written keeping in view the information asked for like price list, mode of payment, discount to be allowed etc. Businessman should reply to the inquiries carefully and promptly.

Specimen of Quotation Letter

Tel. 2531566	M/s virtual	E-mail: virtual@gmail.com
Fax. 9720104030	6/d, C.G mkt.	Website: http://www.virtual.com
Ref. PR/F/2002/27		Dated: July 27,2002

M/s NIS
Chauhan Market
Dehradun
Uttaranchal - 248001

Sub: Your letter No. PR/F/2002/27 dated July 27, 2002

Dear Sir,

Thank you for your letter of enquiry. We would be glad to meet your requirements of selling our fan in your retail showroom.

Our quotations are given in the price list enclosed. We offer 10% discount on order above Rs.50, 000. Besides, we allow a grace period of 45 days for payment of dues to our regular customers.

We are confident that you will find our prices competitive and our terms and conditions reasonable. We look forward to meeting your requirements.

Thanking you,

Yours faithfully,
For M/s Virtual
(V.k.Agarwal)
Sales Manager

IN-TEXT QUESTIONS

I. Which of the following statements about business enquiry letters do you consider to be correct?

(i) By writing these letters, a buyer gets information about the prices of goods.

(ii) In business enquiry letter the writer cannot ask for sample of goods.

(iii) Here the writer doesn't give information about the quantity of possible purchases.

(iv) The seller supplies the relevant information to the buyer through such a business letter.

(v) Letter written in response to business enquiry letter is called Quotation letter.

II **Order Letter:** In the previous section, we have studied about letters of enquiry and reply to enquiry i.e., quotation letter. The prospective buyer after receiving the reply to his enquiry letter may decide to place on order with that business house which offers goods at minimum price and at favorable terms and conditions. Letters written by a buyer to the seller giving the order to purchase the goods is called order letter.

III **Complaint Letter:** A complaint letter is written when the purchaser does not find the goods upto his satisfaction.

It is normally written by the purchaser when he receives wrong, defective or damaged goods or receives incorrect quantity of goods. It can also be written directly to the transit authority when the goods are damaged in transit. Thus, we may define a letter of complaint as the letter that draws the attention of the supplier or any other party on account of supply of defective or damaged goods.

Points to be considered while writing a complaint letter-

- Complaint letters should be written immediately after receiving the defective goods.
- Mistakes as well as difficulty due to mistake should be mentioned clearly
- Proposal to correct the mistakes should be made
- Suggestions on how the complaint should be dealt with, i.e., mention of compensation,replacement, discount, cancellation etc, should be made.
- Mention period in which the corrective action should be taken
- Request to be careful in future.

IV **Recovery Letter:** The letter written by the seller for collection of money for the goods supplied to the buyer is called recovery letter. The aim of recovery letter is to collect money without annoying the customers. The letter should include information regarding the amount of arrears argument for payment, and last date for payment. The language of recovery letter should be polite, so that the customer is not offended and future transactions with him are not adversely affected.

IN-TEXT QUESTIONS

I. Fill in the blanks with suitable words.

(i) On receipt of defective goods, the buyer writes ________ to the seller.

(ii) On finding that the goods have been damaged in transit, the buyer writes complaint letter to ________

(iii) Aim of recovery letter is to ____________ from the buyer.

(iv) Complaint letter is written by ____________ to the ____________.

Recovery letter draws the attention of the buyer towards the ________.

PLANNING THE LETTER

The writer of the letter should have good thinking power and should plan out its contents before writing the letter. It helps in assorting all relevant facts, figures and places so that the letter becomes more useful and result oriented. The following steps are to be taken for planning a letter and they are as follows:

(a) Collecting facts or information: It refers to collecting all the relevant facts or information to be included in the letter.

(b) Selecting right or accurate style: It implies to the initiation of letter and can be done through three approaches or styles. They are:

1. **Direct:** In this type we can jump into main issue or conclusion before giving any type of preface or introduction. For example, Enquiries, Quotations, Orders, etc.

2. **Indirect:** It involves making indirect or preface for the main information, issue or subject.
3. **Persuasive:** It should be written in a way that the reader should be motivated and its content should arouse his interest to create a demand for the business. For example - sales executive offering lucrative offers to sell his products through effective business letter writing.

(c) Arranging Facts, Figures and Places: The collected information of the relevant facts, figures and places should be arranged and assorted properly so that the letter becomes link chain and should be able to satisfy readers.

THE SEVEN C'S OF BUSINESS LETTER WRITING

Effective letter writing boils down to knowing why you are writing a letter understanding your reader's needs and then clearly write what you need to say. Every letter should be clear, human, helpful and as friendly as the topic allows. The best letters have a conversational tone and read as if you were talking to your reader.

In brief then, discover the Seven-Cs of letter writing. You should be

- o Clear
- o Concise
- o Correct
- o Courteous
- o Conversational
- o Convincing
- o Complete

Structure of Business Letter

A business letter is typically composed of the following components:

A Letterhead: The letterhead is the company's logo, and usually exists at the top of the letter for all to see.

Date Drafted: The letterhead is usually followed up by the date of which the letter was drafted.

The Name and Address of the Recipient: A typical example of this would be

Salutation: The salutation refers to how you greet the recipient.

Examples include;

"Dear John" or "Dear Mr Doe".

Alternatively, if you do not know the name of your recipient, you may write;

"Dear Sir/Madam." Use a similar level of formality in your salutation as you would use when talking to that same individual on the phone.

Subject Line: This line indicates what the letter is all about. It indicates the main message of the letter. Good subject lines are concise, and specific as well as appropriately written depending on the contents of the message.

For example, the message line of a positive message should state the good news. A persuasive message should include your stance and some reader benefit for instance. It all depends on the contents as well as the context of the message.

Contents of your message: The message that you would like to communicate to your respondent. It is the purpose of your entire letter.

Complementary Close: This cool sounding name is actually the statement which usually precedes your name in most letters. Examples include "Yours sincerely" or "yours faithfully."

Signature and the Name of the Sender: This section of the letter consists of the signature together with the writer's name as well as his or her designation.

Revising the Letter Writing

Revision is very important in letter writing as it helps you to check out your faults and spelling mistakes.

First Revision: Structure and Clarity

In first revision read quickly your letter to look for logical fallacies, parts of the text that you need to clarify, places where you should include additional information, and organizational and other broad structural changes that need to be made. You can avoid the spelling, punctuation, and similar errors right now. There's no sense in spending a lot of time fixing capitalization and grammar. Instead, think about the overall content of your letter. Determine whether or not the information really suits the scope and purpose of your letter.

Also as you are reviewing your document, revise as needed to make it more cohesive by adding or improving transitions and by tying in new information with old information.

Second Revision:

After you have made any necessary changes to improve structure, organization, coherence, clarity, logic, redundancy, and so forth, then go back and read over your letter more closely. As you read, be on the lookout for spelling, capitalization, punctuation, and grammatical errors, and correct them as needed.

Vocal Revision

After you do the major revising of your letter, it is a good idea to read it out loud. This is an excellent way to notice awkward or less aesthetic passages that you wouldn't necessarily notice from just reading silently. As you read, when you come across something that sounds awkward or stilted or when you stumble over a word or phrase, revise it.

Final Revision

Here, if you notice any major problems in organization or logic that you somehow missed in previous readings, rework your document, if possible. Even if it means asking for more time, it's probably the better option.

Conclusion

Though revising your writing admittedly can take a fair amount of time and effort, the far better results are well worth the effort. Revision is an essential part of the writing process.

Types of Letters

The following are the types of letters:

1. **Persuasive:** This type of letter is used to persuade a person, company, organization, etc., into an action of some sort. This type of letter uses the Block Letter Format. The writer does not know the audience well, but knows their beliefs.
2. **Complaint:** This type of letter is used to lodge a complaint about a product or service. This type of letter uses the Block Letter Format. The writer does not know the audience, but needs to make a case why the product or service is faulty. The letter is very formal and straight to the point.
3. **Application:** This type of letter is used to introduce you to a company or organization in the application of the job. This type of letter uses the Modified Block Letter Format. The writer knows general information about the audience. The purpose of this letter is to "sell yourself" to the reader.
4. **Friendly Letter:** This type of letter is used for friends, acquaintances, pen pals, etc. It is informal in style and type and uses the Simplified Block Letter Format. The writer knows the audience well.
5. **Thank You:** This type of letter thanks someone for services received, gifts, etc. The format for this type of letter depends on how well you know the receiver. A thank you letter to a company would require a more formal format such as Block Format, while a thank you to a friend would suffice with a Simplified Block Format.

EXERCISE

Q.1 What is the importance of letter writing as a skill in today's business environment?

Q.2 What are the components of a good letter?

Q.3 Mention some of the main principles of letter writing.

Q.4 How should you plan a letter?

Q.5 What is the ideal structure of a letter?

Q.6 How many types of letters are there? Explain them.

Q.7 How is revision of a letter important in letter writing?

PART B

What You Have Learnt

- Correspondence plays are important role in our daily life. It is the means through which we exchange our ideas, thoughts and other information with our friends, relatives and other people.
- We know that business operations are not limited to any locality, state or nation. Since businessmen live at distant places they do not have sufficient time to contact their customers personally. This difficulty has been overcome by writing letters. This is a part Business Correspondence.

The importance of Business letters

(i) It helps in maintaining proper relationship

(ii) It is inexpensive and convenient mode of communication

(iii) It creates and maintains goodwill

(iv) It serves as evidence

(v) It helps in expansion of business.

The essential qualities of a Business letter are:

Inner Qualities	Outer qualities
Simplicity	Quality of paper
Clarity	Colour of the paper
Accuracy	Size of the paper
Completeness	Folding of letter
Relevance	Envelope
Courtesy	
Neatness	

The essential parts of a Business letter are:

(i) Heading	(ii) Date
(iii) Reference	(iv) Inside address
(v) Subject	(vi) Salutation
(vii) Body of the letter	(viii) Complimentary close
(ix) Signature	(x) Enclosures
(xi) Copy circulation	(xii) Post script.

The various types of letters are:

- Letter of enquiry
- Quotation letter
- Order letter
- Letter of complaint
- Letter of recovery

TERMINAL EXERCISE

- What is meant by business correspondence?
- How is personal correspondences different from business correspondence?
- Explain the importance of writing a business letter.
- Describe the inner and outer qualities of a good business letter.
- What is meant by Enquiry letter? What are the points one should remember while writing an enquiry letter.
- Explain the various parts of a business letter with the help of a specimen.
- What is meant by Quotation letter? How does it different from enquiry letter?
- What is meant by Recovery letter?
- What is meant by Order letter? Give a specimen of an order letter.
- What is meant by Complaint letter? Under which situations is a complaint letter written?
- State the important points one should keep in mind while writing a complaint letter in business.

ACTIVITY FOR YOU

(i) You want to buy a book from the Navbharat Publication, which is situated at Rajpur road, Dehradun, Uttarakhand - 248001. Write a letter indicating your requirements.

(ii) Suppose you are the owner of a shop that sells ceiling fans. You received an enquiry letter from M/s Virtual Hotels, Connaught Place, Dehradun seeking information about the price and availability of fans. Write a letter in response to the enquiry made by M/s Virtual Hotels.

CHAPTER-12

Oral Communication

Oral skills, both speaking and listening, are at the very foundation of good communication.

Oral communication can be defined as the effective interpretation, composition, and presentation of information, ideas, and values to a specific audience.

On the other hand, oral communication can be significantly more effective in expressing meaning to a person. This distinction between precision and effectiveness is due to the extensive repertoire of signals available to the speaker: gestures, intonation, inflection, volume, pitch, pauses, movement, visual cues such as appearance, and a whole host of other ways to communicate meaning. A speaker has significantly more control over what the listener will hear than the writer has over what the reader will read. For these techniques to be effective, however, the speaker needs to make sure that he or she has the audience's attention.

Some of the examples of Oral Communication are:

Face to face communication, Telephonic Communication, Public Address System (Speech), Informal rumor mill (Grape Wine), Audio & Visual Media(Radio, TV), Lectures, Conference-Interchange of views, Meetings, Cultural Affairs.

Oral communication requires the background skills of presenting, audience awareness, critical listening and body language.

Oral communication can be more personal than written communication. This is the most important aspect of oral communication.

The importance of the use of oral channels of communication varies according to the subject field and branch of engineering. An example of an area where oral communication is of great importance is the construction and building business, where people often work with unique objects and need to solve specific problems in a short space of time. The telephone and tele-facsimile (for the transmission of diagrams etc.) are invaluable tools.

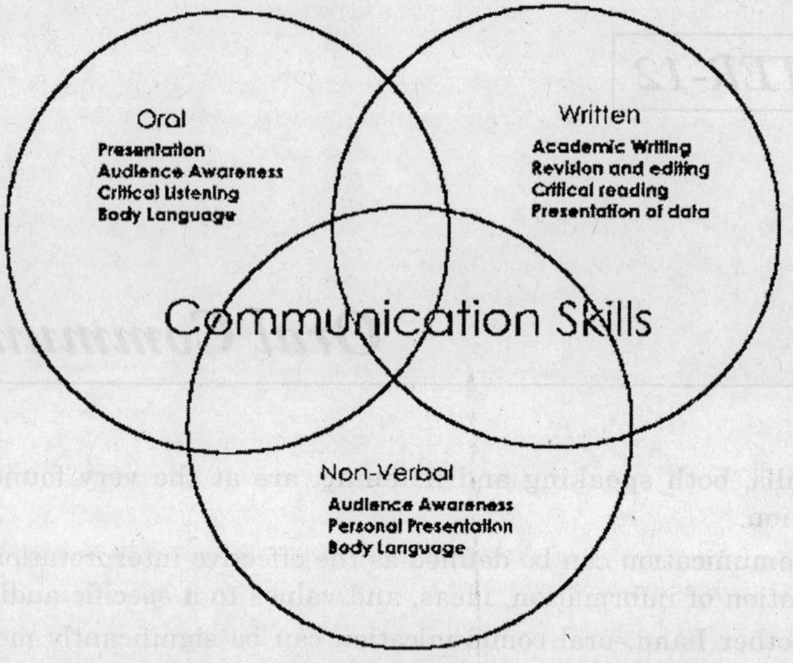

Fig. 12.1

Oral skills – both speaking and listening – are at the very foundation of literacy. Classroom talk helps students to learn, to reflect on what they are learning, and to communicate their knowledge and understanding. The strategies in this section provide simple but powerful tools for improving communication in every classroom and all subject areas. Whatever you teach, these tools can help you to obtain more precise information about what your students know and can do. This, in turn, can help you to provide better feedback and guidance. Students need authentic opportunities to learn how to listen and speak effectively in a variety of situations – in pairs, and in small and large groups.

Students are sometimes assigned an oral activity (e.g., working in small groups) without a clear understanding of what is expected and how to be most effective. By taking the time to teach specific oral strategies in the context of your subject area, you will boost your students' confidence and performance.

STRUGGLING STUDENTS NEED

- Encouragement and explicit instruction to build their strengths and address their needs.
- a safe and encouraging environment to practise oral skills, if English is not their first language.

- extra practice, a peer to work with, and support from the teacher before presenting.
- well-chosen partners or team members who can model knowledge, skills and strategies at a level that is accessible and not intimidating.

Pair work

Working in pairs provides students with an opportunity to "think aloud" about what they know, and a process for acquiring and reflecting on information. For many students, pair work is a comfortable starting point to practise the skills they will need to participate in larger groups.

Small-group discussions

As with pair work, the strategies for small-group discussion give students the opportunity to develop critical thinking skills, build positive relationships, work cooperatively, and participate actively in their learning. You can put your students at ease by modelling effective skills for small-group discussion and by providing many opportunities to practise these skills in a safe environment.

Whole-class discussions

Students learn more readily in a class where they experience cooperation and a sense of belonging. By involving the whole class in shared activities, and by teaching students how to be good listeners, to respect each other and to participate without fear, you can maximize participation and minimize anxiety for all students.

Presentations

Presenting in front of a class can be a terrifying experience. Most students dread the class presentation, especially if they have not had enough instruction or practice before evaluation. By taking time to teach effective presentation skills before such an assignment, you free the student to focus on the content instead of the "performance." The quality of presentations improves with effective instruction, practice and support.

Pair Work: Think/Pair/Share

In this strategy, students individually consider an issue or problem and then discuss their ideas with a partner.

Purpose

Encourage students to think about a question, issue, or reading, and then refine their understanding through discussion with a partner.

Payoff Students will:

- reflect on subject content.
- deepen understanding of an issue or topic through clarification and rehearsal with a partner.
- develop skills for small-group discussion, such as listening actively, disagreeing respectfully, and rephrasing ideas for clarity.

Tips and Resources

- Use Think/Pair/Share in all subject areas for almost any topic. For example: in Business, discuss ethical business practices; in Math, solve a word problem together to better understand the task; in Science, exchange hypotheses before conducting an experiment.
- Use it to help students with their in-class reading. Ask them to read a chapter, think about the ideas, and then take turns retelling the information to a partner.
- Use it at any point during a lesson, for very brief intervals or in a longer time frame.
- Increase the amount of time devoted to Think/Pair/Share, depending on the complexity of the reading or question being considered. This strategy can be used for relatively simple questions and for ones that require more sophisticated thinking skills, such as hypothesizing or evaluating.
- Take time to ensure that all students understand the stages of the process and what is expected of them.
- Review the skills that students need to participate effectively in Think/Pair/Share, such as good listening, turn-taking, respectful consideration of different points of view, asking for clarification, and rephrasing ideas.
- After students share in pairs, consider switching partners and continuing the exchange of ideas.
- See other strategies, including Take Five and Discussion Web for ways to build on the Think/Pair/Share strategy.

Further Support

- Some students may benefit from a discussion with the teacher to articulate their ideas before moving on to share with a partner.

Pair Work: Think/Pair/Share

	What teachers do	What students do
Before	o Have students read a selection or pre- pare a topic, question, or prompt for a planned Think/Pair/Share activity. OR o Choose a "teachable moment" during the class where the process of reflection and shared discussion would bring deeper understanding, and insert a brief Think/ Pair/Share activity into the lesson at that point. In either case: o Consider the social and academic goals for the Think/Pair/Share activity, and plan for pairing of particular learners that would further those goals.	Read the chapter or section, if the hink/Pair/Share is based on information and ideas from a reading selection.
During	o Ask students to spend several minutes thinking about and writing down ideas.	Formulate thoughts and ideas, writing them down as necessary to prepare for sharing with a partner.
	o Set clear expectations regarding the focus of thinking and sharing to be done.	o Practise good active listening skills when working in pairs, using techniques such as paraphrasing what the other has said, asking for clarification, and orally clarifying their own ideas.
	o Put students in pairs to share and clarify their ideas and understanding. o Monitor students' dialogue by circulating and listening.	
After	o Call upon some pairs to share their learning and ideas with the whole class.	Pinpoint any information that is still unclear after the pair discussion, and ask the class and teacher for clarification.

- o Possibly extend the Think/Pair/Share with a further partner trade, where students swap partners and exchange ideas again.
- o Consider adding a journal writing activity as a productive follow-up to a Think/Pair/Share activity.

In pairs, students take five minutes to orally review a concept and present it to the class, usually at the beginning or end of a class period.

Purpose

- Briefly consolidate or reinforce learning.

Payoff

Students will:

- Develop a strategy that can be used to review content material in all areas.
- Share responsibility for teaching and reviewing with each other.
- "Talk" their way into meaning and understanding through verbal rehearsal.
- Perceive continuity with content from class to class, especially when a lot of material is being covered quickly.

Tips and Resources

- o Use this review-and-share strategy on a regular basis to reinforce the learning of subject-specific vocabulary.
- o Have the take-five pairs present their reviews on sheets of chart paper, which you can then post in the classroom for ongoing review.
- o Try not to pair students who are too far apart in their ability or understanding of the material.

Further Support

- o Students may benefit from pairing with a partner who speaks the same first language so that they can clarify the concepts in their first language and build more confidently on their prior knowledge.

Pair Work: Think/Pair/Share

What teachers do	*What students do*
Before	
o Decide on a concept from the previous day's lesson for review and consolidation	

o Arrange students in "take five" buddies, with a designated student A and student B in each pair.	
During	
o Invite students to engage in a Think/ Pair/ Share with their partner on a concept, formula, term, etc., from the previous day's work, assigning a diffe- rent task to the A and B students. (For example, student A recalls or checks notes to find the formula for the vol- ume of a cone, while B does the same for the formula for the volume of a sphere. Each shares the formula with his/her partner. Or student A reviews the process of photo- synthesis, while B checks the meaning of all the words /terms in the process.)	Review notes, texts, and other materials relating to the concept being discussed o Consolidate learning through sharing, discussing, and clarifying the concepts together. o Plan how to present the concept to the class if called upon to do so.
o Let students know that one pair will be responsible for reviewing the concept with the whole class.	
After	
Ask one pair to write the formula/ process or concept on the board and review it with the class.	Support each other as a team in recalling and explaining the details to the class.
o Repeat the process, if appropriate, by rearranging the pairs and setting another Think/Pair/Share task for review and discussion.	o Practice and develop the skills of explaining, rephrasing, and clarifying for the class.

In this strategy, students practice their listening and speaking skills. Students divide into pairs and take turns speaking, listening, and retelling information in timed steps.

Purpose

- o Enhance critical thinking skills.
- o Create an argument and be concise in its delivery.
- o Develop attentive listening skills while sharing viewpoints on an issue.
- o Make connections between written and oral skills.

Payoff

Students will:

- o share ideas
- o develop listening skills.
- o apply skills in different ways - in pairs, small groups, and with the whole class.

Tips and Resources

- o Timed Retell can be informal or more formal, as described here. In the more formal approach, students require more confidence.
- o Students may make notes during the brief presentations given by their partners.
- o It is possible to use this activity with more extensive subject matter. In that case students will need time to properly research the topic and devise their arguments.
- o Additional information about peer editing is found in Writing Strategies: Revising and Editing.

Further Support

- o The struggling student may feel uncomfortable speaking in front of the whole class. Students should be given other opportunities to share and practise speaking skills before this assignment.
- o As always, consider pairs carefully.

What teachers do	*What students do*
Before	
Choose a relevant question or issue that might invite debate.	Individually brainstorm and jot down ideas about both sides of the question or issue.
o Make sure that students have the appropriate background knowledge on the issue.	
During	
Put students in pairs, facing each other.	Decide who will be partner A and who will be partner B.
o Direct all partner A students to begin by speaking on the "for" side of the issue. Partner A will talk for one minute, while partner B listens.	o Partner A speaks for one minute, convincing partner B as much as possible.

o Ask partner B to retell the talk for one minute	o Partner B listens carefully and retells partner A's argument.
o At the end of one minute, ask partner B to present the opposing side of the argument.	o Partner B wraps up the retell and then gives the opposing argument.
o Direct partner A to then retell partner B's argument.	o Partner A listens carefully and retells partner B's argument.
After	
o Invite students to write each other's side of the issue into a paragraph or letter to the editor.	Write a carefully constructed paragraph from the partner's point of view.
Put students into groups of four. Each group should contain students who all argued from the same point of view in their paragraph.	o Read the paragraph to the partner to ensure that no important details have been omitted.
Ask students to read their paragraphs to the other members of their group. Organize the class in a circle to discuss the group findings.	o Peer-edit paragraphs for sentence structure, grammar and mechanical errors. Read their paragraph to the other members of the group. o Comment on the points discussed in each reading. o List the common points. Present the list of common points to the class, ensuring that all group members have a chance to speak.

SMALL-GROUP DISCUSSIONS: GROUP ROLES

Students are divided into groups of a certain size - for example, five members. Each student is assigned a specific role and responsibility to carry out during the small-group discussion.

Purpose

- o Encourage active participation by all group members.
- o Foster awareness of the various tasks necessary in small-group discussion.
- o Make students comfortable in a variety of roles in a discussion group.

Payoff

Students will:

- o All speak in small groups.
- o Have specific roles to fulfill, clearly defining their role in the small group.

- o Receive positive feedback that is built into the process.
- o Participate actively in their learning.

Tips and Resources

- o It is important to vary the composition of small groups, allowing students the opportunity to work with many classmates of various abilities, interests, backgrounds, home languages, and other characteristics.
- o It is a good idea to repeat this activity throughout the year. This will allow students the opportunity to experience different roles and to improve their skills.
- o Time the exercise to keep students focused on the task.
- o If research is required, involve all students in the process, regardless of their role. This activity provides an excellent way for students to share research and come to a consensus about important information.
- o For role ideas, see Student/Teacher Resource, Sample Role Cards.
- o To encourage students to reflect on their learning, use Student Resource, Small-group.

Discussion Reflection Sheet

Further Support

- o Although it's important to vary the composition of groups, it is also important to consider the particular needs of struggling students.

What teachers do	*What students do*
Before	
o Choose the task or topic for discussion.	o Understand the question/task.
o Decide how many students will be in each group.	o Understand their roles and responsibilities.
o Decide on the roles for each group member.	
o Prepare role cards for each student. See Student Resource, Sample Role Cards.	
o For example: Leader: defines the task, keeps the group on task, and suggests a new way of looking at things. Manager: gathers and summarizes materials the group will need, keeps track of time, and collects materials the group used.	

Note maker: Record ideas generated by the group and clarifies the ideas with the group before recording.

Reporter: reports the group's ideas to the class.

Supporter: provides positive feedback for each speaker, makes sure everyone gets a turn, and intercepts negative behavior.

During

- o Divide the class into groups.
- o Present the parameters of the task.
- o Explain time limits and keep track of time.
- o Circulate around the room, ensuring that all students are fulfilling their roles.
- o Comment constructively on the group process.

- o Fulfill the roles to the best of their abilities.
- o Use active listening skills.
- o Act positively and encourage other group members.
- o Participate fully in the discussion.
- o Adhere to the time limits set by the teacher.

After

Ask students to individually complete an evaluation of the discussion. See Student Resource, Small-group Discussion Reflection Sheet.

- o Put students in groups.
- o Debrief with the whole class, asking students to comment on the success, benefits of the exercise.
- o Plan to repeat this activity, allowing students to try each of the other roles.

- o Complete the Small-group Discussion Reflection Sheet.
- o Discuss the successes and benefits of using structures/ rules in small groups.

Sample Role cards

LEADER

- o Does everyone understand what we're doing?
- o Have you thought about this in another way?
- o We're getting off topic; let's get back to the task.

MANAGER

- o Here are the materials we'll need. This is what I think we should look at.
- o We have ________ minutes left.

- o Now that we're finished, let me gather the materials.

NOTE MAKER

- o Would you repeat that so I can write it all down?
- o What do you mean by that?
- o Let me read to you what I've written so far.

REPORTER

- o Let's review the secretary's notes.
- o Does anyone have anything to add before I report to the class?
- o Does anyone have any suggestions on how to report to the class?

SUPPORTER

- o Really good point.
- o We haven't heard from __________ yet.
- o Please don't interrupt; you'll get a turn.

Small-group Discussion Reflection Sheet

Name:______________________________________

Role: ______________________________________

Topic:______________________________________

Comment on your group's ability to work together in a positive manner. Consider cooperation, listening, and organization.

What are your group's strengths?

What are your group's areas for improvement?

Comment on your own ability to work in a positive manner. Consider cooperation, listening, and organization.

What are your strengths?

What are your areas for improvement?

Comment on your success in fulfilling the role you were assigned

Sol. In this easy-to-use strategy, students are divided into small groups, gathered around a piece of chart paper. First, students individually think about a question and write down their ideas on their own section of the chart paper. Then students share ideas to discover common elements, which can be written in the centre of the chart paper.

Purpose

- o Give all students an opportunity to share ideas and learn from each other in a cooperative small-group discussion.

Payoff

Students will:

- o Have an opportunity to reflect and participate.
- o Have fun interacting with others and extending their learning while accomplishing the task.

Tips and Resources

- o The strategy can be used with a wide variety of questions and prompts.
- o Use the place mat strategy for a wide range of learning goals, for example:
  - To encourage students to share ideas and come to a consensus on a topic
  - To activate the sharing of background knowledge among student
  - To help students share problem-solving techniques in mathematics and science
  - To take group notes during a video or oral presentation.
- o Groups of 2 to 4 are ideal for place mat, but it can also work with up to 7 students in a group.
- o You may choose several questions or issues for simultaneous consideration in a place mat strategy. To start, each group receives a different question or issue to work on. Once they have completed their discussion, the groups rotate through the various questions or issues until all have been explored. using structures/ rules in small groups.

Further Support

- o Give careful consideration to the composition of the small groups, and vary the membership according to the students' styles of learning and interaction, subject-matter proficiency, and other characteristics.
- o Some students may benefit from being able to "pass" during group sharing.

What teachers do	*What students do*
Before	
o Divide students into groups of 4 or 5.	
o Decide on a question for the students to answer.	
o Distribute chart paper to each group.	
o Ask the students to divide the chart paper into sections equal to the number of students in the group, leaving a circle or square in the centre of the chart.	

During	
o Direct each group member to think about, then write silently about a question or topic in their personal area of the chart paper for a determined amount of time.	o Gather their thoughts about the chosen question or topic and write silently in their own area of the paper, respecting the space and silence of all members of the group
After	
o Give a signal for students in each group to discuss their ideas and experiences and find the common elements or ideas.	o Take turns sharing ideas with the group.
o Have students post the charts to share their group's thinking with the class.	o Engage in discussion with all group members to arrive at common elements or ideas.
	o Record common ideas in the centre of the place mat.
	o Use oral skills, such as active listening, requesting clarification, and coming to consensus.
	o Circulate around the room to look at the ideas on the charts of other groups.

EXAMPLE

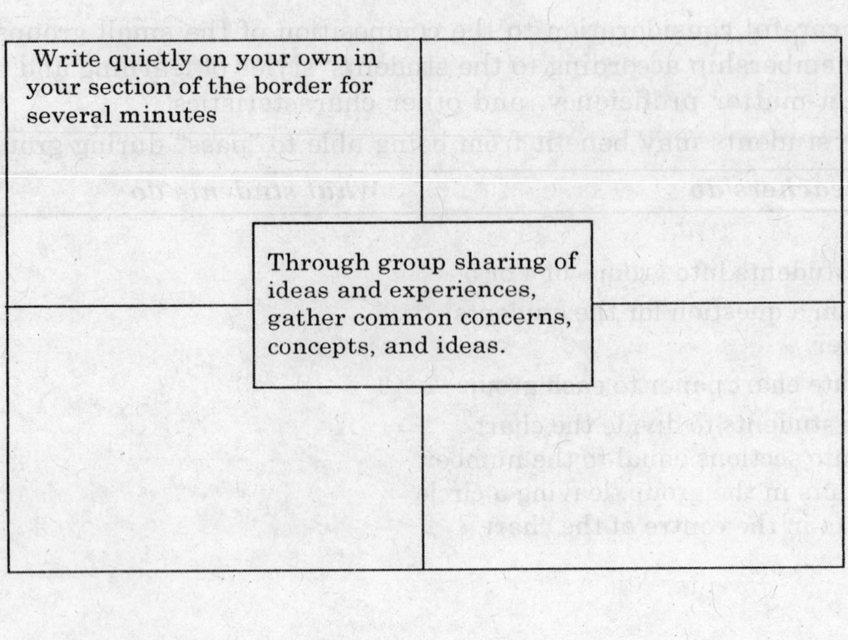

Example: Take a few a few minutes to about and individually write down you know about the (activating students' Freedoms. knowledge) and Freedoms. Charter of Rights and background (activating students' background knowledge)

it protects people's rights
all people should be equal
federal government

guarantees equality of men &
women freedom of religion
freedom of the press
equality for the people with
disabilities

Religious Freedom
EQUALITY
All people have rights

Equality for all Canadians
people have rights

freedom to protest against the govt.

it affects our laws
gives everyone the right to practice
their religion
federal or provincial I'm not sure

Small-group Discussions: Determining Key Ideas

In this strategy, students work individually to identify three to five key ideas. In pairs, they then share ideas and streamline their list of key ideas down to two to four. Finally, two pairs of students combine to share and reduce further to one or two key ideas.

Share and consolidate learning when reading new material.

Students will:

- Understand a topic more deeply.
- Share learning with peers.
- sharpen skills in small-group discussion, especially in listening and persuading.
- learn to focus on the "big ideas."
- practise how to summarize ideas.

Tips and Resources

- Use this strategy at the end of a chapter or series of readings to help students summarize the key ideas of the unit.
- Vary the pairing of students so that they learn to work with different partners.
- To help students visualize the process, use Student/Teacher Resource, Steps for Working
- Together to Determine Key Ideas.

Small-group Discussions: Determining Key Ideas

What teachers do	*What students do*
Before	
o Provide students with blank cue cards or stick-on notes.	Read and keep notes of main ideas.
o Assign a reading selection.	o Make judgments on what the three to five key ideas of the reading might be.
o Have students complete an initial summary of the reading in class or for homework before beginning the strategy.	o Summarize the key ideas on three to five separate cards or stick-on.
o Direct students to write three to five key ideas from their reading, one per cue card or stick-on note.	
During	
o Instruct students to form pairs to discuss their key ideas and to narrow these to two to four cards per pair.	o Discuss the key ideas in pairs. Through negotiation, streamline them to two to four ideas per pair. Write the two to four combined ideas on cards.
o Then, have two pairs of students then work together to further negotiate and refine their key ideas to one or two entries only.	o Combine with another pair to further engage in give-and-take to condense the key ideas to a maximum of two.
o If appropriate, review the language of negotiation and polite persuasion with students, in preparation for the negotiation process (e.g., Do you think...? Would you agree that...? I don't agree with that because...).	o Continually evaluate their own understanding of the material and its main ideas as they engage in the negotiation process.

After

- Call upon each group to report their summaries of the most important ideas to the whole class.
- Share the selected most important ideas with the whole class.

Steps for Working Together to Determine Key Ideas

On your own, summarize three to five key ideas and stick - on them.

↓

In pairs, share your key ideas and, through discussion, streamline them to two to four ideas between you.

↓

In a group of four, discuss and further trim your list of key ideas to one or two, to be shared with the class.

Discussion Etiquette

These are some of the etiquette rules that you may wish to have on your class list. Although this list should be created by students, you may want to guide them to ensure your class list is complete.

- Participate fully.
- Take turns speaking - one person speaks at a time.
- Let others know that you have not finished speaking by using phrases such as I have one more thing to add, furthermore, in addition, etc.
- Wait for your turn - don't interrupt.
- Use supportive gestures and body language:
  - Maintain eye contact with the speaker.
  - Nod to show you are listening.
  - Use encouraging facial expressions.
  - Don't use inappropriate gestures.

- Use respectful phrases when disagreeing with another speaker.
- Listen carefully and attentively to other speakers.
- Encourage and support those around you.
- Avoid sarcasm and put-downs.
- Remain open to new ideas.
- Use inclusive language.
- Ask questions when you don't understand.
- Don't monopolize the conversation.

Speaking Out

Phrases for respectful disagreement include:

(i) I disagree with... because...
(ii) I can't agree with... because...
(iii) On the other hand...
(iv) I doubt that because...

Examples of inappropriate disagreement include:

I. You're wrong.
II. No way!
III. Come on!
IV. What!
V. That's crazy/stupid/ridiculous.
VI. Are you kidding?
VII. I hate that.
________ doesn't know what he/she's talking about.

Phrases for politely expressing an opinion include:

(i) In my opinion...
(ii) I believe...
(iii) I think...
(iv) Personally, I feel...
(v) Not everyone will agree with me, but...

Phrases for politely making suggestions include:

(i) Why don't you/we ...
(ii) How about...
(iii) Why don't we/you try...

(iv) One way would be...
(v) Maybe we could...
(vi) I suggest we...

Presentations: Presentation Modeling

Many students are hesitant to give presentations in class; they are uncomfortable or nervous and do not clearly understand what an effective presentation looks like. By demonstrating an ineffective presentation, modeling an effective presentation, and facilitating student collaboration, teachers will ease student stress and clearly define an effective presentation.

Purpose

- o To clearly define exemplary presentation skills.
- o To create a comfortable, safe environment in which students may be successful in presentations.

Payoff

Students will:

- o collaborate with each other and the teacher to improve the teacher's ineffective presentation.
- o experience, first hand, examples of ineffective and effective presentations.
- o observe their suggestions for improvement in action.

Tips and Resources

- o Teachers may consider modelling only the effective presentation. Teachers need to be cautious when demonstrating the ineffective presentation - a sense of humour goes a long way to help your students be comfortable.
- o It may be helpful to videotape both the teacher's first presentation and the improved presentation so that students may re-examine the changes.

Further Support

- o Give careful consideration when determining pairs of students who will present together.

What teachers do	*What students do*
Before	
o Prepare a brief presentation for the class that demonstrates ineffective presentation skills.	o Observe teacher's first presentation and prepare to comment on areas in need of improvement.

During	
o Ask students to write down all of the things that needed improvement in the presentation.	Write down all areas needing improvement.
o Divide class into small groups.	o Discuss ideas with small group, compiling one list to be presented to the class.
o Facilitate whole-class discussion about the areas needing improvement.	o Present ideas for improvement to the class.
o Discuss how these improvements might take place.	o Observe improved presentation.
o Prepare a new presentation for the class, making improvements suggested.	o Write down further suggestions. Discuss with the class how these suggestions may improve their own presentations.
After	
Distribute Effective Presentation Skills.	Add any new ideas to their handouts.
o Facilitate class discussion - is anything missing that needs to be added?	o Prepare presentations
o Give students a topic for their presentations.	o Practice presentations.
o Divide class into pairs - these pairs will give each other constructive criticism as they prepare to present.	o Work in pairs throughout practice sessions to give each other constructive criticism and helpful hints.
	o Before presenting, use handout as a checklist to ensure their presentations are effective
	o Present to class.

Effective Presentation Skills	√
Is the topic presented clearly and logically?	
Is the presentation clearly organized with an introduction, middle, and conclusion?	
Does the speaker have a thorough knowledge of the subject?	
Did the speaker gather information from a variety of sources?	
Did the speaker use visual aids to support the presentation?	
Did the speaker use appropriate tone and language for a classroom presentation?	
Did the speaker use effective eye contact with the audience?	
Did the speaker talk fluently without false starts?	

Did the speaker vary the volume of speech?

Did the speaker vary the rate of speech?

Did the speaker articulate clearly?

Did the speaker use conjunctions effectively?
(e.g., and, then, because)

Did the speaker explain unfamiliar terms to others?

Did the speaker talk for the appropriate amount of time?

Did the speaker avoid unnecessary movements such as shuffling, toe tapping and shaking?

Did the speaker involve the audience in the presentation?

Did the speaker engage and inspire the audience?

Present

How can I improve my presentation skills?

- Understand and explain your content.
- Organize with a beginning, middle, and end.
- Emphasize key ideas (repeat, rephrase).
- Use strong, convincing language.
- Use visual aids.
- Repeat, rephrase key ideas.
- Practice.
- Prepare for questions.
- Communication

Q.10 What do you understand by Group Dynamics? (May-2007)

Ans. Groups are the basic building blocks of organizations. It is now very common for groups of employers to make decisions to solve difficult problems that were once the domain of authoritarian incentives. Given below are the characteristics of Group personality:

1. Spirit of conformity
2. Respect for group values
3. Resistance to change
4. Group prejudice
5. Collective power

Q.11 What do you understand by 'Group conflicts'? How shall these be managed effectively? Explain. (November 2007)

Ans. Group conflict: Group conflict is an 'express struggle' between two inter-dependent parties who perceive incompatible goals, scarce resources and interference from the other party in achieving their goals. There are two aspects in relation to conflict:

1. Expression: The two sides must communicate/express about the problem for there to be conflict.
2. Perception: Conflict evolves perceptions in the two sides may only perceive that their goals, resources, and interference are incompatible with each other's. Managing conflicts: The climate in which conflict is managed is important. It is essential to plan communications to foster a supportive climate, marked by emphasis on:

- Presenting ideas or options
- Problem orientation- focusing attention the task
- Spontaneity - Communicating openly and honestly
- Empathy - understanding another person's thoughts.
- Equality- asking for opinions
- Willing to listen to the ideas of others.
- Successfully managed conflicts can be constructive and can strengthen relationships in an organization.

Q.12 What is meant by "Negotiation"? Name the various steps which can be identified in the process of negotiation from start to the completion of the process. (November-2008)

Ans. When two or more persons meet together and talk/ discuss on any business or non business matter, it is known as negotiation. When same persons discuss specific proposals in order to come to a mutually accepted solution; whether it is with an employer, family member or business partner, it can be said that negotiation is a common way of settling things in business.

Steps in the negotiation process

- Preparing
- Arguing
- Signaling
- Packaging
- Bargaining
- closing and arguing

Oral Communication

- Expressing ideas and information as well as influencing others through the spoken word

- o Can also include nonverbal communication
- Important for any career, whether you use it in informal conversations or business presentations
- Key Concepts: speaker, message, channel, receiver, feedback, noise, context

Three Elements of Oral Communication

- Content: information conveyed in presentation
- Organization: structure of presentation
- Delivery: means of communication

The advantages of oral communication are:

1. **Saves time:** In a situation where time is of essence, oral communication will be the best even if it is an oral communication. This is especially true in situations where split second decisions have to be made in the workplace. The authorities may just give an oral communication. This has to be obeyed by the subordinate who is carrying out the activity. There may be no time for the written order to be signed and passed on to the person doing the job.
2. **Face to face interaction:** When two people communicate in an office, face to face communication will be a lot more personal in nature. There may be a communication between a manager and a person who is being laid off from work. A personal face to face communication will at least try to take away the sting from the lay off. If the same person was given a written communication, it may be more difficult for the person to digest the loss of job.
3. **It can be recorded:** Due to the various advantages in the electronic and communication devices, an oral communication can be recorded either as a voice message or even as a video recording. This communication can be used from time to time in different places.
4. **Oral communication does not need writing skills:** Written communication needs the person who is communicating to have language skills and also writing skills as it will be a record of the communication. In oral communication, the person does not need any formal writing skills to get the message across to the people who are receiving the communication.
5. **Oral communication can be on the spot:** Written communication has the disadvantage in the fact that there should be at least a paper and pen for written communication. In oral communication, there does not need to be any such things and it can be on the spot. Oral communication can be spontaneous unlike the written communication.

Public Speaking

Public speaking is the process of speaking to a group of people in a structured, deliberate manner intended to inform, influence, or entertain the listeners.

Purpose of Public Speaking

The purpose of public speaking can range from simply transmitting information, to motivating people to act, to simply telling a story. Public speaking has several components as motivational speaking, leadership/personal development, business, customer service, large group communication, and mass communication. It can be a powerful tool to use for purposes such as motivation, influence, persuasion, informing, translation, or simply entertaining.

Points to remember in Public Speaking

Get Attention

In public speaking a content rich speech is one of the factors in keeping the audience's attention. But even with a great speech their attention can wander but with some application you can maintain and arrest their attention.

Be energetic

Energy should be there in delivery. Speak with variety in your voice. Slow down for a dramatic point and speed up to show excitement. Don't just stand behind the lectern, but move a step away to make a point. When you are encouraging your audience, take a step toward them. Gesture to show how big or wide or tall or small an object is that you are describing. Show facial expression as you speak. Smile when talking about something pleasant and let your face show other emotions as you tell about an event or activity. Whatever your movements, they should have purpose.

Eye contact

Eye contact is very important in public speaking. If it is a small audience, you can look at each person in a short period of time. If it is a large audience, look at the audience in small "clumps" and move from one clump to another. One way to insure good eye contact is to look at your audience before you start to speak. Go to the lectern and pause, smile, look at the audience, and then speak. This will help you maintain good eye contact throughout your presentation as well as commanding immediate attention.

One of the ways to have consistently good eye contact is not to read your speech. Use note cards that have key words on them. The word or phrase should trigger the thought in your mind and then you can speak it. If you are including a quotation or complex statistics, reading from your note card actually lends credibility. If you write out your speech you will tend to read it and lose eye contact with the audience, as well as not being as enthusiastic in delivery as when you speak from note cards.

Use Pauses

In public speaking, as with conversation, your audience will almost always react to silence. It quickly increases their attention. Use a pause when you wish to emphasize a particular word or idea. A pause gives the audience time to digest your point before you move on. It also provides a "breather" for your audience as it is hard work to be attentive when being spoken to non-stop.

State facts in an interesting way

Facts can be dull and they are cold; they do not touch the listener's heart. Listeners will quickly lose interest if bombarded with them. However, facts add weight to your speech. Use facts that are clear concrete and interesting. State them in a way that makes them easy to grasp e.g. don't say: The death rate in China is high, instead use, Every time you breathe someone in China dies.

Visual aids

Using visual aids or holding things up will make your speech more interesting and gain the audience's attention. Select aids that make your ideas clear vivid and effective. For an article to be used at best advantage it must be able to be clearly seen by everyone. The objects used should make good sense and be in line with the points being made. Listeners like visual aids because they deliver variety from too many words.

Use of Relevant Stories

People like stories. They have grown up listening to and watching them. To be effective the story should relate to your message. Start your story in a way that engenders anticipation, participation or curiosity, e.g. No-one will talk about this for publication but.... Keep the story brief, you want to leave the audience wanting more. To add more interest use conflict, dramatic action or suspense in the story.

"Wow" factor

Include a "wow" factor in your speech. Something in your speech should make your audience think, "Wow!" It could be a story, a dramatic point, an unusual statistic, or an effective visual that helps the audience understand immediately. With a "wow" factor, you then have something to look forward to in the speech that you know will have an impact on your audience.

Humor

Consider using a touch of humor in your speech. Humor will help you to be perceived as an amiable person, and it is hard for people to disagree or be bored if they are smiling at you. Until you have lots of experience, keep your humor short. Perhaps inject a one-liner or a quotation.

Tell a short embarrassing moment in your life that you might have thought not funny at the time. Now which make you laugh at the experience. Avoid long stories or jokes. Probably the least risky use of humor is a cartoon. The cartoon is separate from you and if people don't laugh, you don't feel responsible.

Body Language

Body language is a form of non-verbal communication, which consists of body posture, gestures, facial expressions, and eye movements.

It includes facial expression, eye contact, postures, gestures, touch.

An understanding of and ability to use gestures, expressions and non-verbal cues to help communicate a message (for example, using changing the tone and volume of your voice to convey emotion and feeling, or controlling posture and nervous gestures to present confidence).

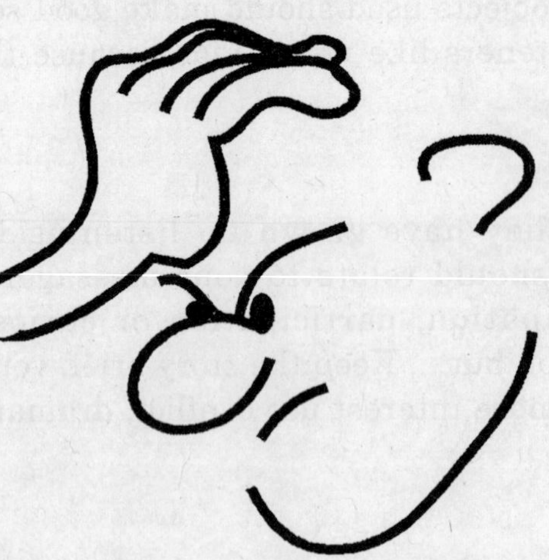

Fact: Up to 93 % of communication is non-verbal

Body language may provide clues as to the attitude or state of mind of a person. For example, it may indicate aggression, attentiveness, boredom, relaxed state, pleasure, amusement, and intoxication, among many other cues.

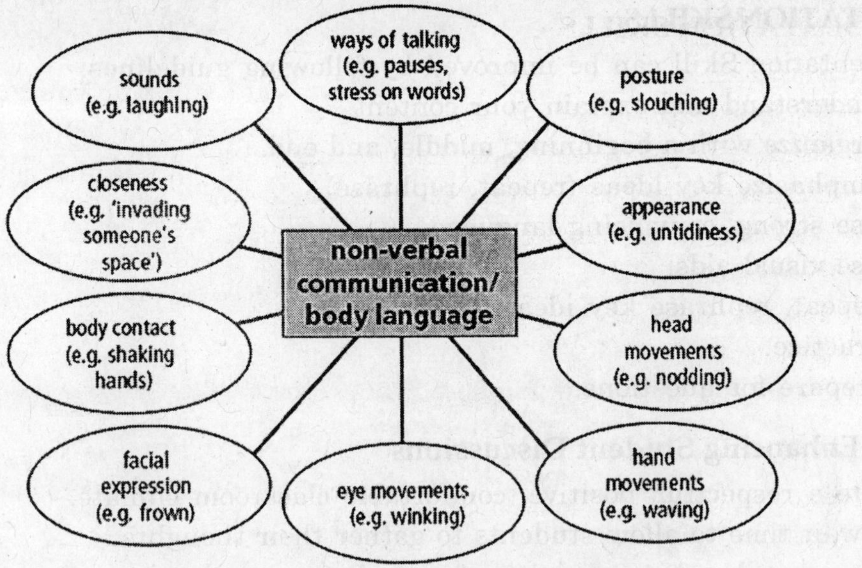

Fig.12.2: Different forms of body language

Physical expressions like waving, pointing, touching and slouching are all forms of nonverbal communication. The study of body movement and expression is known as kinesics.

Let us see some of the body language gestures that will help in interpreting body language.

Body Language Gesture	*Meaning*
Brisk and Erect walk	This body language means confidence.
Person walking with hands in pockets, shoulders hunched	This body language shows a person in dejection.
Person tapping or drumming with his fingers	This body language means that the person is impatient.
Person standing with hands on hips	This body language means readiness and aggression.
Person with prolonged tilted head	Indicates boredom.
Pulling or tugging the ear	The person is indecisive.
Someone biting nails	This is a proof of insecurity and nervousness.
Person looking down, face turned away	Just means disbelief.
Hands clasped behind back. apprehensive.	The person is angry, frustrated and
Person sitting with legs crossed, foot kicking slightly	This body language means boredom.

PRESENTATION SKILLS

Presentation Skill can be improved by following guidelines:

- Understand and explain your content.
- Organize with a beginning, middle, and end.
- Emphasize key ideas (repeat, rephrase).
- Use strong, convincing language.
- Use visual aids.
- Repeat, rephrase key ideas.
- Practice.
- Prepare for questions.

Tips for Enhancing Student Discussions

Create a respectful, positive, comfortable classroom climate.
Add wait time to allow students to gather their thoughts.
Rephrase and restate questions for students.
Encourage students to elaborate and give them time to do so.
Ask pointed questions.
Restate the students' points to confirm and clarify them.
Call on other students to extend their classmates' responses.
Use praise that gives specific feedback.
Give students many opportunities to practice speaking.
Limit teacher talk to maximize participation by students.

FACTORS AFFECTING PRESENTATION SKILLS

I. Effective Listening : These are some of the etiquette rules that you may wish to have on your class list. Although this list should be created by students, you may want to guide them to ensure your class list is complete.

1. Participate fully.
2. Take turns speaking - one person speaks at a time.
3. Let others know that you have not finished speaking by using phrases such as I have one more thing to add, furthermore, in addition, etc.
4. Wait for your turn - don't interrupt.
5. Use supportive gestures and body language:
   - Maintain eye contact with the speaker.
   - Nod to show you are listening.
   - Use encouraging facial expressions.
   - Don't use inappropriate gestures.

6. Use respectful phrases when disagreeing with another speaker.
7. Listen carefully and attentively to other speakers.
8. Encourage and support those around you.
9. Avoid sarcasm and put-downs.
10. Stay on topic.
11. Remain open to new ideas.
12. Use inclusive language.
13. Ask questions when you don't understand.
14. Don't monopolize the conversation.

INTERVIEWING SKILL

The basic approach to an interview is to be well prepared. This means two things - preparing yourself practically for the interview, and gathering knowledge and information you can draw on during the interview.

Points to remember for an interview:

- Be sure you know the time, date and location of the interview and name of interviewee where appropriate.
- Plan to reach the interview location no earlier than half an hour before the interview time, anticipate delays.
- Decide what you are going to wear ready in advance.
- Do not go to the interview laden down with baggage - psychological as well as physical.
- Take the bare minimum of belongings necessary.
- Concentrate on the interview at the interview nothing else.
- If you are asked to bring certificates, references etc, get them ready before the day.
- Take your interview letter.
- On arrival ensure the receptionist knows you are there; visit the toilets to tidy up etc.

Interviews vary tremendously, from very informal to formal. However, some questions can be anticipated, as can the subject matter. If you are well prepared, then the majority of problem questions should not arise. You should know about the company, you should know about yourself and you should have a good idea of the demands of the job - these questions will not be a problem to the well prepared interviewee.

A few general rules for interviews:

Speak up when answering questions.

Answer briefly, but try to avoid yes or no answers.

Don't worry about pausing before you answer, it shows you can think and are not spitting out the sound bites you learned!

Don't worry about admitting you don't know - but keep this to minimum.

Don't embellish answers or lie! Be as honest as possible.

Be prepared for hypothetical situation questions; take your time on these type of questions.

Be prepared for the unexpected question, that's designed to see how you cope with the unexpected.

How to control your body language in an interview?

- Sit comfortably with both feet on the floor, lean slightly towards the interviewer.
- Don't play with your hair or you hands. Keep them out of pockets.
- Do not try to create defensive barriers between you and interviewer, like a brief case on your knees, folded arms or crossed legs....even if you feel you need to.
- Maintain natural eye contact with the interviewer but don't stare at the interviewer.
- If there's more than one interviewer, look at who's talking.
- When you're talking, shift your glance from one to the other.
- Don't over use your hands, if you are a natural gesticulator.
- Don't squirm and fidget.
- Do nod and Mmm, to show you're listening to them.
- Above all try to be you, try to be natural, unless you're naturally offensive!

Types of interviews

1. **Unstructured Informal Interview:** The unstructured informal interview is normally conducted as a preliminary step in the interview process. Such interviews are entirely informal and are not controlled by a specific set of detailed questions. Rather the interviewer is guided by a pre-defined list of issues. These interviews amount to an informal conversation about the subject. The respondent is encouraged to talk freely about the subject, but is kept to the point on issues of interest. The respondent is encouraged to reveal everything that he/she feels and thinks about these points. The interviewer must note (or tape-record) all remarks that may be relevant and pursue them until he/she is satisfied that there is no more to be gained by further probing.
2. **Structured Interview:** A structured interview follows a specific questionnaire and this research instrument is usually used as the basis for

most quantitative surveys. A structured questionnaire is administered where specific questions are asked in a set order and in a set manner to ensure no variation between interviews.

Respondents' answers are recorded on a questionnaire form during the interview process, and the completed questionnaires are most often analysed quantitatively. The structured interview usually denies the interviewer the opportunity to add or remove questions, change their sequence or alter the wording of questions.

3. **Indepth Interviews:** Indepth interviews are one-to-one encounters in which the interviewer makes use of an unstructured or semi-structured set of issues to guide the interview process. The object of the exercises is to explore and uncover deep-seated emotions, motivations and attitudes. They are most often employed when dealing with sensitive matters and respondents are likely to give evasive or even misleading answers when directly questioned. Most of the techniques used in the conduct of indepth interviews have been borrowed from the field of psychoanalysis. Indepth interview are usually only successful when conducted by a well trained and highly skilled interviewer.
4. **Telephonic Interviews:** A telephonic interview has potential in the field of businesses, government agencies and other organisations or institutions. Even then, it is still the case that telephone surveys are rarely without bias. Telephonic interviews afford a certain amount of flexibility. It is possible, for example, for interviewers to put complex questions over the telephone. The interviewers can probe, skip questions that prove irrelevant to the case of a particular respondent and change the sequence of questions in response to the flow of the discussion, and earlier replies can be revisited. The interaction between interviewer and interviewee that is possible over the telephone simply is not achievable through a mailed questionnaire. In comparison to personal interviews, telephone interviews do not appear to enjoy any margin of advantage. Perhaps the only advantages are those of speed and cost.

Some important guidelines for the interviewer:

If the interviewer wants to be effective, the interviewer must adhere to six fundamental rules. These are:

- Must avoid appearing superior or condescending and make use of only familiar words.
- Must put question indirectly and informatively.
- Must remain detached and objective.
- Must avoid questions and questions structure that encourage 'yes' or 'no' answers.

- Must probe until all relevant details, emotions and attitudes are revealed.
- Must provide an atmosphere that encourages the respondent to speak freely, yet keeping the conservation focused on the interview.

Case Study

An Indian marketing executive from a start-up company recently came to us because he gave many webinars and his audience wasn't responding well.

Problem: He spoke too fast and didn't leave pauses between his words, so that his English was very hard to understand.

Solution: He became much more conscious of his speech patterns once we videotaped him and analyzed how he sounded. We made a list of the words he uses in his sales pitches and presentations and laid them out phonetically for him to practice during work hours, especially on the phone. He kept a sign next to the phone that said" slow down" and made sure that he followed through with every call he made.

EXERCISE

Q.1 What is meant by a 'structured interview'?

Q.2 What do you understand by unstructured interview?

Q.3 How many types of interviews are there? Explain them.

Q.4 What is meant by oral communication?

Q.5 What are the components of oral communication?

Q.6 How can you conduct an effective presentation?

Q.7 What is the importance of body language in business communication?

Q.8 How are gestures important in you communication process?

Q.9 What are the factors affecting presentation skill?

Q.10 What are the points which should be considered by an interviewer while taking interview?

CHAPTER-13

Report Writing

Report writing is an important task. It is essential for communication, which is necessary for maintaining transparency.

After thorough study, collection of all relevant facts and information and proper scrutiny and analysis of a problem relating to past or present, submission of the conclusions supported by statements and other relevant data, etc. is called a report, which offers suggestions for solution of the problem studied.

Definition of Report

According to British association for commercial and industrial education, a document in which a given problem is examined for the purpose of conveying information and findings, putting forward ideas first and sometimes making recommendations.

Features of a Good Report

- It should be factual and not imaginative.
- Objective should be free from any personal opinion, bias, prejudice and criticism.
- It needs to be structured in an orderly manner.
- It should be concise and complete.
- It should contain all important information and details.
- It should be logical and accurate.

Process of Report Writing

1. Selecting

(*a*) Simplify, and be ruthless about it. Reject the irrelevant, agonize over the doubtful, and make sure you've got the essential.

(*b*) Justify your conclusions with facts, and state their sources. Build the facts into a logical and consistent case, so as to lead the reader to the same conclusions as your own.

2. **Planning the structure:** The facts themselves should therefore be a set of directions, which will lead and guide your reader along a route. This route has to be planned *before* you write your report, perhaps as follows:
   - First, divide it into major sections. Every subject can be broken down in this way, and the headings will probably become the headings in your report.
   - Make a list under each heading of all the points you would like to mention. Note the information that you'll need to support them.
   - Now mark the most important points, the essential steps in your reasoning.
   - Next, mark the least important ones, points your reader would find irrelevant. These you will probably reject.
   - Lastly, arrange the points in a final, logical sequence, so as to meet your objective. Some people write them out on scraps of paper at this stage, and shift them around until they get the order right.

Format of Report Writing

The format will depend upon the type and purpose of the report, its intended readers, and the conventions of presentation and layout prescribed by the organisation in which you are operating. In general, there are two broad types of format which are differentiated by whether the summary and/or recommendations are placed after the main body of the report, or are placed earlier, before the main body. The eventual format chosen might be a combination or a condensed version of these two formats.

A format where the findings/recommendations follow the main body

Cover sheet

Title page

Abstract

Table of contents

Introduction

The body of the report

Conclusion (and recommendations if applicable)

References / Bibliography

Glossary (if needed)

Appendices

A format where the findings/recommendations precede the main body

Letter of transmittal

Title page

Table of contents
Summary and/or recommendations
Body of report
Conclusions
Appendices
Bibliography

3. Structure of a Report: The structure of a report is made up of some main parts which are as follows:

(*a*) Title page

It contains the title, sub-title if any, date, author's name and position, and distribution list. It may also carry a reference number or other classification. It should not overcrowd the page. It should present a clear, simple layout of the report.

(*b*) Contents list

The contents of short reports may be shown on the title page-or not at all. More extensive ones should always have a separate page, listing the major sections or chapters, sub-sections if any, and appendices, and giving their page numbers. It should be laid out clearly so as to show the relationship between them.

The Contents of the report should be consistently laid out throughout the report and you should include both page numbers and title numbers.

The contents page sets out the sections and subsections of the report and their corresponding page numbers. It should clearly show the structural relationship between the sections and subsections. The conventions for section and page numbering are as follows:

Number the sections by the decimal point numbering system:

1.0 Title of first main section (usually Introduction)
1.1 First subheading
1.2 Second subheading
2.0 Title of second main section
2.1 First subheading
2.2 Second subheading
2.2.1 First division in the second subheading
2.2.2 Second division in the second subheading
3.0 Title of third main section

(*c*) Summary

The summary should include a gist of all of the key points. It should be attractively written and stimulate the reader to read the whole thing.

The summary provides a brief overview of the substance of the report; usually no more than half a page. It is not an introduction to the topic. The summary should outline all the key features of the report, including the topic, what you did and how you did it, and the main outcomes of your work. This is the most important part of the report which should be written in the last.

The summary

- reflects the topic of the report
- outlines the approach
- gives the most important findings of the research or investigation, or the key aspects of the design
- states the main conclusions.

The summary does not

- provide general background information
- explain why you are doing the research, investigation or design
- refer to later diagrams or references.

(*d*) Introduction

This gives the background to the report, and shows why it was necessary. It states the objective of the report, who called for it, and the scope and treatment.

The introduction should tells why the report is being written. Reports are mostly always written to solve a business problem. Reports maybe commissioned because there is a crisis or they maybe routine.

It is usually half to three-quarters of a page in length. The purpose of the introduction is to set the context for the report, provide sufficient background information for the reader to be able to follow the information presented, and inform the reader about how that information will be presented.

The introduction includes

- the background to the topic of the report.
- a clear statement of the purpose of the report, usually to present the results of the research, investigation, or design.
- a clear statement of the aims of the project.
- technical background necessary to understand the report; e.g. theory or assumptions.

(*e*) Body of the report

It is the main part of the report. This contains the detailed facts and findings, shows how they were arrived at, and indicates the findings and conclusion to be derived from them.

The introduction and conclusions act as a frame for the body only: therefore all the details of your work must be included in the appropriate section. The presentation of information should flow logically so that the reader can follow the development of the report. It is also essential that you choose concise but informative headings and subheadings so that the reader knows exactly what type of information to expect in each section.

The body of the report

- presents the information from the research, both real world and theoretical, or your design
- organises information logically under appropriate headings
- conveys information in the most effective way for communication:
- uses figures and tables
- can use bulleted or numbered lists
- can use formatting to break up large slabs of text.

(*f*) Conclusions

Conclusion draws out the main points of the report and presents a considered judgment on them. It provides an effective ending to the report. The content should relate directly to the aims of the report as stated in the introduction, and present the essential features of the report. This part of the report:

- states whether you have achieved your aims
- gives a brief summary of the key findings or information in the report
- highlights the major result of the report and their significance.

The conclusions should summarize the findings of the report and should not include diagrams or graphs in this area. This area should be short, clearly follow the order of the findings.

(*g*) Recommendations

All reports should include recommendations or suggestions. It is always best if this can be directly linked, but may not always be possible. The recommendations should clearly follow what is said in the conclusions.

(*h*) Appendices

Some reports need detailed supporting information or perhaps information that only some readers need. All this is included in the appendices. It contains material that is too detailed to include in the main report, such as raw data or detailed drawings. The conventions for appendices are as follows:

- each appendix must be given a number (or letter) and title;

- each appendix must be referred to by number (or letter) at the relevant point in the text.

(*j*) Bibliography and/or References

This section of the report includes the books and articles consulted as a basis for the report, or those you want to suggest as further reading or both. There are two parts of the references:

- citations in the text of the report
- a list of references in the final section

A citation shows that information comes from another source. The reference list gives the details of these sources. You need to use in-text citations and provide details in the references section when:

o information is incorporated from other sources; e.g.:

o factual material

o graphs and tables of data

o pictures and diagrams

o you quote word-for-word from another work (when you do this the page number must be given in the in-text citation)

Glossary

This can be a help if your readers include non-experts as well as experts. Here you need to define any technical terms given in your report.

Types of Reports

Reports can be classified in the following two forms:

According to function

According to formality

According to functions the reports may be divided into three parts

- Informational reports
- Analytical reports
- Research reports

According to formality the reports may be divided into two parts:

- Statutory reports
- Non statutory or voluntary reports

The above two may further be divided into two parts again, i.e. (i) routine reports and (ii) special reports.

1. **Informational reports:** These reports present facts about certain given activity in detail without any note or suggestions. Whatever is gathered is reported without giving any thing by way of either explanation or any suggestion. Generally such reports are of routine nature. A company registrar asking for allotment return within the stipulate period is nothing but informational routine, falling under statutory but routine report.
2. **Analytical reports:** These reports contain facts along with analytical explanations offered by the reporter himself or may be asked for by the one who is seeking the report. Such reports contain the narration of facts, collected data and information, classified and tabulated data and also explanatory note followed by the conclusions arrived at or interpretations. A company chairman may ask for a report on falling trends in sale in a particular area. He will in this case be naturally interested in knowing all the details including that of opinion of any of the investigator.
3. **Research reports:** These reports are based on some research work conducted by either an individual or a group of individuals on a given problem. Indian oil company might have asked its research division to find some substitute for petrol, and if such a study is conducted then a report shall be submitted by the research division detailing its findings and then offering their own suggestions, including the conclusions at which the division has arrived at as to whether such a substitute is these and if it is there can the same be put to use with advantage and effectively. All details shall naturally be asked and has to be given. In fact such a report is the result of a research.
4. **Statutory reports:** These reports are presented according to the requirements of a particular law or a rule. The auditor reports to company registrar has to be submitted as per the requirements of country legal requirement. A return on compensation paid to factory workers during a period by a factory has to be submitted to competent authorities periodically. These reports are generally prepared in the prescribed form as the rules have prescribed.
5. **Non statutory reports:** These reports are not in the nature of legal requirements or rules wants, therefore, the reports are to be prepared and submitted. These reports are required to be prepared and submitted:
   (*i*) for the administrative and other conveniences
   (*ii*) for taking decision in a matter
   (*iii*) for policy formulations
   (*iv*) for projecting the future
   (*v*) anything alike so that efficient and smooth functioning maybe assured and proper and necessary decision may be taken with a view to see that

everything goes well and the objectives of the organization are achieved with assured success.

6. **Routine reports:** These reports are required to be prepared and submitted periodically on matters required by the organization so as to help the management of the organization to take decisions in the matters relating to day to day affairs. The main objectives of routine reports are to let the management know as to what is happening in the organization, what is its progress where the deviation is, what measures have been taken in solving the problems and what to do so that the organization may run smoothly and efficiently. Routine reports are generally brief. They only give the facts. No comments or explanations are usually offered in such reports. Generally forms are prescribed for preparation and submission of such reports.

7. **Special reports:** Such a type of report is specially required to be prepared and submitted on matters of special nature. Due to an accident a death of the foreman has occurred in a factory. The factory manager may ask for a detail report from the head foreman. Such a report is classified as special reports. These reports contain facts and details and may contain suggestion, comments and explanations as well.

<u>Steps towards writing of Different Types of Business Reports</u>

The writing process includes all the activities-thinking, writing, discussing and revising-that take place while writing a business report. There are mainly five steps in the process of writing effective business reports.

Step 1: Collect your ideas

Ideas for your report will come to you in pre-written forms, such as words, thoughts, mental images, jottings, sketches and point form outlines in your head.

Collect your thoughts and ideas with:

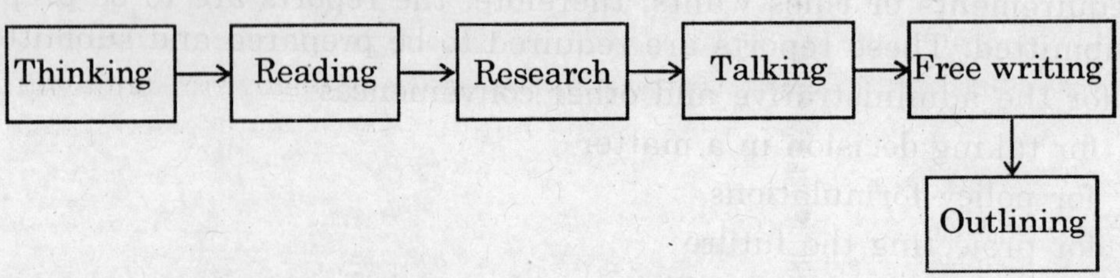

Think about reasons of writing a report. Organize your thoughts with an outline map.

First, collect all the information you need. Then outline what you need to say in your report. Then arrange what you need to say in the order that you want to say it. Outlining is one of the most important parts of the report-writing process. Outlining saves you time and helps your reader.

Step 2: Write a first draft

The drafting stage of the writing process is when you start the report writing.

Your first attempt at writing the whole report is called the draft report. Before beginning to write your first draft, place your research plan where you can easily refer to it and organize all the information you have collected into sections corresponding to the plan. You don't need to include title page, table of contents or summary at this stage. Begin by writing, going straight to writing up your research findings.

Make the draft as fast as possible, concentrating on its content, expressing accurately the research and including everything you want to say. It's likely that once you start, ideas will come pouring out. If you come to a standstill, leave that part for now and go ahead to another section.

- get your ideas down on paper
- think while you write
- write to discover what you want to say
- ignore spelling mistakes, grammar, style and organization for now
- write as much as you can
- revise your draft after writing

Step 3: Revise your draft

This is the most important stage in the report writing. Think of your reader and re-write as needed to write to his level. Make two or three revisions, preferably over days or weeks instead of all in one day.

First, work on the big ideas

- re-structure sections
- re-organize major sections
- add or remove ideas
- move blocks of text
- number ideas
- bullet points

Then, work on the minor details

- remove unnecessary words
- remove clichés

- polish your sentences
- make sure your paragraphs follow one another

Step 4: Editing

In editing mistakes are find out that escaped your attention. In this stage cover the complete text and read line by line to find the mistakes.

Step 5: Final Writing

Lay out your report in a style that is both attractive and easy to read.

Style of Report Writing

Style of the report is the way or manner you convey your thoughts to other people.

Writing style is probably the most individual aspect of a report, but again there are useful guidelines which aid the readability, professionalism, objectiveness and impact of a report. A report can be presented in an effective style by following some guidelines as given below:

(*a*) Write the first draft. Don't evaluate what you are writing; simply break the spell of that blank, white sheet of paper.

(*b*) Then edit your draft, reading it through the eyes of your reader. In particular, clear up any clichés and obvious ambiguities, eg, '. . . the flooding was caused by the liquidation of the contractors working on the sewage system.' substitute short, simple words where appropriate, eg, 'start' for commencement', and 'end' for 'termination'.

Write in simple language; choose words familiar to your reader. Technical terms are useful shorthand to use with fellow specialists, but simply cloud the issue for anyone else.

Use active, rather than passive verbs, e.g, 'The Board has approved this project,' rather than 'Approval has been given by the Board for this project.'

Presentation of a report

You may need to use tables, graphs, bar charts, or other diagrams.

Set your report out generously. Use wide margins; space out paragraphs; and indent sub- headings.

Summary

Effective Report Writing

- To produce a good report requires effort
- The content must be clear, concise and accurate!
- Above all it must convey an image of total professionalism

- Great effort goes into the preparatory work but the 'look' of the document should not be forgotten
- We can't write your report for you
- But we can help you to produce a document which is worthy of all your hard work!

Format

- Your report needs a good Format and structure – it should include most of the following categories:
  - o Heading Page
  - o Content List
  - o Executive Summary
  - o Background / Introduction
  - o Methods
  - o Results
  - o Observations
  - o Conclusions and Appendices

Heading Page

- Leave the Report heading page 'til last!
- The report header needs a lot of thought & first impressions count when looking at a report
- It's the secret to making a simple report look absolutely brilliant! The header is fun to create!
- Think about the Layout of the front page:
  - o Size and Style of font
  - o Colour of font (the bigger the font enables you to use a lighter colour)
  - o Use of images and logos

Contents Page

- This is obviously another page you will leave until you have compiled the main body of the report
- A contents list is only necessary for a lengthy report
- Give each section of your report a title and cross refer this to a page number

Executive Summary

- An Executive Summary is a real 'must' if your report is a really lengthy one
- An executive summary provides bullet points of all of the main elements of your report

- It gives the 'reader' a snapshot view of the contents
- It ensures that your main points are emphasised
- And it conveys a really professional image!
- An executive summary is easy to create once you have written the complete report

EXERCISE

Q.1 What do you understand by a report and what are the features of a good report?

Q.2 Explain the process of report writing.

Q.3 What should be the structure of a report?

Q.4 How many types of reports are there?

Q.5 Explain the body of a report and what is its importance in report writing?

Q.6 Describe the routine reports, statutory reports.

IMPORTANT QUESTIONS

Q.1 What is communication

Q.2 Differentiate between verbal and non verbal communication.

Q.3 When written orders are issued?

Q.4 What is formal communication?

Q.5 What is informal communication?

Q.6 What is grapevine?

Q.7 Differentiate between grapevine and rumor.

Q.8 How can telephone be effectively used?

Q.9 Differentiate between Fax and E-Mail.

Q.10 What is teleconferencing?

Q.11 What is meant by communication barriers?

Q.12 What is the role of listening in communication?

Q.13 Why positive attitude is important in communication?

Q.14 What is information technology?

Q.15 What is WWW?

Q.16 How internet is connected?

Q.17 Why is listening important in business communication?

Q.18 How can listening be made effective?

Part B

Q.1 "Communication is as essential for a business concern as blood and breathing are for life". Do you agree? Explain.

Q.2 What do you mean by formal communication? Discuss its advantages and disadvantages.

Q.3 What is downward communication? Discuss the purpose, pre-requisites, potential benefits and problems of downward communication.

Q.4 What is upward communication? Discuss its advantages and disadvantages. How can it be made effective?

Q.5 What is horizontal communication? Differentiate it with upward and downward communication.

Q.6 What is grapevine? Discuss its various types, advantages and disadvantages. How can it be made effective?

Q.7 "One should feed, water and cultivate the grapevine rather than to curb its growth." Explain.

Question 7

What is meant by 'Emotional Intelligence' and 'Emotional Quotient'? State any six social competencies associated with Emotional Intelligence. (May-2007)

Answer

Emotional Intelligence: Emotional intelligence refers to the capacity to recognizing your own feelings and those of others, for motivating yourself, and for managing emotions well in yourself and in your relationships. It describes abilities distinct from but complementary to academic intelligence, the purely cognitive capabilities measured by IQ. Many people who are look smart but lack emotional intelligence end up working for people who have lower IQs than they but who excel in emotional intelligence skills.

Emotional quotient inventory is designed to measure a nature of constructs related to emotional intelligence. EQ is the ability to make and deeper connections at three levels: with ourselves (personal mastery), with another person (one-to-one) and within groups/teams. Our EQ or emotional intelligence is the capacity for effectively recognizing and managing our own emotions and those of others. The wonderful thing about EQ, unlike IQ which stabilizing when a person is round 18 years of age is that it can change.

A person today with a low EQ score on 'empathy' can have a higher 'empathy' score in the future – if that person recognizes his/her limitation changes attitude, adopts a learning strategy, and practices key listening and empathy skills.

Social competencies associated with emotional intelligence are as follows:

Social Awareness

1. **Empathy:** Sensing others emotions, understanding their perspective and taking active interest in their concerns.
2. **Organizational awareness:** Leading the currents decision, networks and politics at the organizational level.
3. **Service:** Recognizing and meeting follower, client or customer needs.

Relationship Management

1. **Inspirational leadership:** Guiding and motivating with a compelling vision.
2. **Influence:** wielding a range of tactics for persuasions.
3. **Developing others:** Bolstering others' abilities through coaching, feedback and guidance.
4. **Change catalyst:** Initiating managing and leading in a new direction.
5. Conflict management resolving disagreements.
6. **Building bonds:** Cultivating and maintaining a web of relationships.
7. **Teamwork and collaboration:** Cooperate and team building.

SAMPLE PAPER I
CASE STUDY

An Indian marketing executive from a start-up company recently came to us because he gave many webinars and his audience wasn't responding well.

Problem

He spoke too fast and didn't leave pauses between his words, so that his English was very hard to understand.

Short Answer Questions

1. Give the meaning of Non-Verbal Communication.
2. What is Business Communication?
3. Importance of a business letter.
4. Kinds of Reports.
5. Grapevine communication.

Long Answer Questions

1. What do you understand by the term 'communication'? What are the main features of effective communication?
2. Draft a condolence message to the wife of one of your colleagues expressing sympathy over her husband's death.
3. Explain different forms of written communication.
4. Draft a report of the experts on raising additional capital of the company.
5. Write an essay of about 300 words on *any one* of the following:
   (*i*) Automated Teller Machine (ATM)
   (*ii*) Inflation
   (*iii*) NRI investment in India
   (*iv*) Role of computers.

SAMPLE PAPER II
CASE STUDY

A French executive frequently had to give presentations to senior executives in his company.

Problem

His English was excellent, but because of his heavy French accent, he was often misunderstood. He used gestures that made him look wildly excited and distracted listeners from what he was saying. Furthermore, his presentations had many busy tables, and his messages were confusing and unclear resulting in twelve to eighteen bullet points per slide instead of the six to eight that people can absorb. He relied on his PowerPoint to do the presentation for him instead of speaking freely and persuasively.

Short Answer Questions

1. State, with reasons in brief, whether the following statements are correct or incorrect.

(*i*) Communication is a circular process.

(*ii*) Verbal communication means oral communication.

(*iii*) Your business card says volumes about you.

(*iv*) The formal channel of communication is also called 'grapevine'.

Long Answer Questions

1. What is communication? Explain how communication is an important function of management.
2. What are the barriers of communication?
3. Differentiate in detail between oral and written forms of communication.
4. Distinguish between formal and informal reports. What are the steps involved in report writing?
5. Discuss the following.

(*a*) Importance of communication in business organizations

(*b*) Media of communication

(*c*) Process of communication

(*d*) Audio-visual communication

(*e*) Listening skills

(*f*) g. Formal or official letter structure

(*h*) Information Technology use in communication.

III (*a*) Discuss the application of Johari Window model of communication in organiztions in detail.

Or

(*b*) Differentiate between Intrapersonal and Interpersonal forms of communication?

IV (*a*) Describe various barriers of communcation.

Or

(*b*) Discuss in detail about Gateways of communication for effective communication.

V (*a*) Explain the precautions to be taken for writing good and bad news reports.

VI (*a*) Explain the dos and don't's of oral presentations.

Or

(*b*) Discuss about the increasing use of computers in communication in the society and business as well.

(*a*) Draft a covering letter to be sent along with your resume to Hindustan Levers Ltd., Post Box No.1008, New Delhi-110 001 for the post of sales representative in response to an advertisement in the Times of India. (Prepare only the body of covering)

(*b*) You have to dispatch a letter to Minerals and Metals Trading Corporation's Iron and Steel Division's Manager – Manish Kala. The Corporation is in New Delhi (PIN Code 110003). The office is located at Lodi Road's PSU Complex's Building – Scope Tower. The Iron and Steel Division is on the 5th floor.

Q.1 Explain the layout of a business letter with an example.

Q.2 What are the points to be remembered while drafting an order refusal letter?3. Explain the principles underlying an insurance contract.

Q.3 Explain the principles underlying an insurance contract.

Q.4 Explain the seven C's of communication.

Q.5 Explain the barriers to listening.

Q.6 Discuss the different types of interview in an organization.

Q.7 Explain the types of communication.

Q.8 What is business letter? Explain various types of Business letter.

Q.9 State five objectives of Communication.

Q.10 Draft a letter to Nisha & Co., Madras requesting him to send the latest price catalogue.

Q.11 Explain the various types of report.

Q.12 Write a letter to "The National Insurance Company" informing them about a fire accident.

Glossary

"A"

Active listening

Feeding back the literal meaning or the emotional content or both so that the speaker knows that the listener has heard and understood.

Advertising

Those forms of PR and marketing communication aimed at the influencing and /or promoting purchasing behavior with regard to the services and products of the organization.

"B"

Body language

Nonverbal communication conveyed by posture and movement, eye contact, facial expressions, and gestures.

Brainstorming

A method of generating ideas by recording everything a person or a group thinks of, without judging or evaluating the ideas.

Business learning

Business learning is a specific methodology for education of professionals. It differs from the methods used in the formal education system as adults learn best when

- Learning is accomplished through dialogue
- They feel respected as responsible self directed learners
- They feel their knowledge and experience are valued and can be shared
- They feel able to trust, sense safety in the learning environment
- They see how the skill or information is relevant to their lives or their work
- When they see that the information or skill is immediately useful in performing tasks or to deal with problems they confront in their lives.

Branding

Branding is the use of texts and or images to create a specific image and positive associations for a person, organization, product or service.

"C"

Corporate Communications

Refers to the central communications function led by the SVP, Corporate Communications and Community Partnerships. The UK/US Corporate Media Teams are part of this organization.

Corporate Information

The information on the organization has three functions: disclosing, performing a public service, and acting as an instrument to support organizational policies or programmatic objectives.

Citation

Attributing a quotation or other idea to a source in the body of the report.

Capacity building

'Capacity building is the creation of an enabling environment with appropriate policy and legal frameworks, institutional development, including community participation (of women in particular), human resources development and strengthening of managerial systems. Capacity building is a long-term, continuing process, in which all stakeholders participate (ministries, local authorities, non-governmental organizations and water user groups, professional associations, academics and others.

Capacity building

Activities which strengthen the knowledge, abilities, skills and behaviour of individuals and improve institutional structures and processes such that the organization can efficiently meet its mission and goals in a sustainable way.

Communication

Communication is an activity in which a sender transmits a message, with or without the aid of media and vehicles, to one or more receivers, and vice versa. The way in which communication takes place is referred to as the communication process. The ideal form of communication is a two way process aimed at mutual understanding, sharing of values and action.

Communication plan or strategy

A communication plan or strategy sets the communication goals, chooses the right media and messages and sets out the method of evaluation.

- One first analyses the management or biodiversity issue one wants to address.
- The second step is to analyze what communication obstacles have to be addressed to reach or change the relevant stakeholders.

- The third is to define for each group of stakeholders one needs to communicate to (the target group) the communication objectives, the messages and the means.

Communication objectives

Communication objectives are different from the organization, policy, project or program objectives. Communication as an instrument for the organization, policy, project or program may have the following objectives: setting agenda, forming opinions, raising awareness or creating involvement, generating support, changing knowledge, changing attitudes, changing behavior.

Corporate communication

A management instrument that is used to harmonies all forms of communication in such a way that the Ministry acquires and/or retains the image it wishes to acquire and/or retain among its target groups and customers (both internal and external). Two key concepts in relation to corporate communication are image and identity. In successful organizations corporate communication is a priority of the top executives.

"D"

Diffusion

Diffusion is a process by which an innovation is communicated through certain channels over time among members of a social system. The members of a social system are on the basis of innovativeness classified in 5 groups: innovators, early adaptors, early majority, late majority, laggards behind. Each group needs a different marketing communication approach. The diffusion process contains five steps: knowledge, persuasion, decision, implementation, conformation and adoption or rejection.

"E"

Editing

Checking the draft to see that it satisfies the requirements of good English and the principles of business writing. Unlike revision, which can produce major changes in meaning, editing focuses on the surface of writing.

Education

Education is a set of processes that can inform, motivate and empower people to support biodiversity conservation, not only by making lifestyle changes, but also through promoting change in the way that institutions, business, and governments operate.

External communication

All forms of communication that is geared towards external target groups. There are two types of external communication: press communication (or media relations) and communication aimed at the general public or specific external target groups.

"F"

Formal report

A report containing formal elements such as a title page, a transmittal, a table of contents, and an abstract.

Focus group

A focus group is a non-directive type of interviewing a specific social group. It is a technique in commercial and social marketing. It draws on group interaction to gain greater insight into why certain opinions are held.

Formal communication

Formal communication in general is exchange of information that adheres to the rules and standards that apply to the formal relation between organizations or between the organization and the individual.

Formal Education

Formal education is the hierarchically structured, chronologically graded educational system running from primary through the tertiary institutions.

Framing

Framing is a process of selective control over the individual's perception of media, public, or private communication, in particular the meanings attributed to words or phrases. Framing defines how an element of rhetoric is packaged so as to allow certain interpretations and rule out others.

Feedback

Provides essential information about your success in communicating the message.

"G"

Grapevine

The informal informational network in an organization, which carries gossip and rumors as well as accurate information.

Groupthink

The tendency for a group to reward agreement and directly or indirectly punish dissent.

"H"

House style

The house style of an organization is the codification of the rules how to communicate externally. A house style manual contains standards with regard to logo, colours, lay out, typography etc. in all forms of written communication. It also contains procedures and standards for oral communication and organizational behavior.

"I"

Informal meetings

Loosely run meetings in which votes are not taken on every point.

Internal report

Reports written by employees for use only in their organization.

Interview

Structured conversation with someone who is able to give you useful information.

Introduction

The part of a report that states the purpose and scope of the report. The introduction may also include limitations, assumptions, methods, criteria, and definitions.

Image

(Corporate) Image is the way a person or organization is actually perceived by the outside world (clients and take holders). The corporate image is the result of the actions and behavior of an organization and its staff.

Information

Information is the deliberate and systematic transfer of knowledge by means of processed facts and data aimed at opinion forming or decision making.

Informal communication

Informal communication in general is exchange of information on a personal basis and adheres less to the rules and standards that apply to the formal relation between organizations or between the organization and the individual.

Informal Education

Informal education is the process whereby every individual acquires attitudes, values, skills and knowledge from daily experience, such as family, friends, peers and media. Intermediaries.

Internal communication

All forms of communication within an organisation. Internal communication has a strong link with the corporate culture. It is geared towards the interests both of the organization and of its staff. It takes the form of both formal and informal communication.

Interpersonal communication

All forms of communication involving direct interaction between two or more people. It is the opposite of mass communication. Inter personal communication is highly appreciated by the "receivers". It satisfies their needs of acknowledgement. Tools are visits, phone calls, interviews, informal meetings, personal letters.

Identity

(Corporate) Identity is the way an organisation wishes to be perceived by the outside world. T he corporate culture is an essential part of the corporate identity.

"K"

Knowledge management

The set of disciplined and systematic actions that an organization takes to derive the greatest value from the knowledge it acquires, creates, stores, shares and uses.

Knowledge networking

The process of sharing and developing knowledge through human and computer networks. Knowledge resulting from people sharing information with one another formally or informally. It often occurs within disciplines (such as programmers communicating with one another) and projects (such as all of the people working on a new software product sharing information with one another).

"L"

Letter

Short document using block or modified block format that goes to readers outside your organization.

Lobbying

Lobbying or public affairs are a specialized form of public relations. It refers to those activities aimed at building up and maintaining informal relations with formal decision- makers. The informal relations are used to influence decision making processes in the interest of the organization, its program and/or objectives.

"M"

Memo

Document using memo format sent to readers in your organization.

Message

The message of communication is the content one sends to the receiver. In communication planning one formulates the message in terms of the desired residue of the communication in the mind of the receiver.

Marketing

Those corporate activities aimed at systematically identifying, satisfying and creating the needs of current and potential market parties. The optimal form of marketing is a mix of product, price, place and promotion (marketing communication). Marketing is connected with continuous research of the market, the current and potential customers.

Marketing communication

Those strategic activities – based on research of trends, target groups and/or customers - to promote the services or products of an organisation based on such principles as "perception is the only reality", "it is better to be first than to be best", "exclusivity is better than imitation" and other principles of trends in society. The communication is aimed at acquiring a top brain position for the brand or product. The core business of an organization influences the major choices of marketing communication strategy, as a consumer oriented business has a different market than a business to business operation. A nature conservation fund has a different market than a nature conservation research institute.

Maslow's hierarchy

Maslow's hierarchy of needs Maslow's hierarchy of needs is often depicted as a pyramid consisting of five levels: the four lower levels are grouped together as deficiency needs associated with physiological needs, while the top level is termed growth needs associated with psychological needs. While our deficiency needs must be met, our being needs are continually shaping our behaviour.

Mass communication

All forms of external communication which are theoretically accessible to everyone, as use is made of mass media and mass communication vehicles. The characteristics of mass communication are that it reaches a large number of people at the same time; it is easy for the receiver to ignore the message; it is not possible to customize the message for individual receivers; it is difficult to obtain feedback; it is relatively cheap per receiver reached.

"N"

Nonverbal communication Communication that does not use words.

Paraphrase: To repeat in your own words the verbal content of what the previous

Networking

Networking consists of exchanging information and establishing personal connections.

People networking

People network in many different settings: on the telephone, in hallways, in company lunchrooms, at professional conferences, at trade shows, company meetings, classrooms, lounges, hallways, elevators, airplanes, trains, busses, hotel lobbies and waiting rooms. Some networking is carefully planned and some just happens.

Networking is friendly

Networking is friendly, low-key and essential in our complex society. Advance their careers, advance their own business, to increase their impact on the world and to improve their social lives.

Non Formal Education

Non formal education is organized educational activities outside the established formal system, intended to serve an identifiable learning clientele with identifiable objectives.

Networking examples

This can be e.g. professional updating courses organized by professional associations, trade unions, women's organizations, NGOs etc.

"P"

Process of communication

All forms of communication, both internal and external, which are designed to ensure that a policy-making, program, project or management plan development process proceeds as smoothly as possible and that through an optimal involvement of major stakeholders the final result can count on a maximum of support.

Process or interactive communication

Communication in this sense is an integral part of the process. Tools are hearings, round tables, focus groups, workshops, electronic discussion groups, telephone interviews, live shows on mass media, excursions, etc.

Product or policy communication

All forms of communication, particularly external, which are designed to put across a policy or organizational product (policy proposals, documents, projects) as favorable as possible.

Public affairs

Public affairs or lobbying are a specialized form of public relations. It refers to those activities aimed at building up and maintaining informal relations with formal decision- makers. The informal relations are used to influence decision making processes in the interest of the organization, its program and/or objectives.

Public awareness

Public Awareness brings the issues relating to biodiversity to the attention of key groups who have the power to influence outcomes. Awareness is an agenda setting and marketing exercise helping people to know what and why this is an important issue, the aspirations for the targets, and what is and can be done to achieve these.

Public participation

Public participation is an approach for governments, organizations and communities around the world to improve their decisions by involving those people who are affected by those decisions.

Public relations (PR)

The PR of an organization is aimed at systematically promoting its objectives and priorities. PR aims to realize mutual understanding between the organization and its main clients, other stakeholders and target groups. PR uses free, paid or sponsored publicity. It is based on the principle "be good and tell it" or "be good and let others tell it".

PR tools

PR tools are advertising, new letters, websites, brochures, gimmicks, etc. The relation management is often supported by a specialized information system, which contains

"R"

Report Writing

Report writing is an important task. It is essential for communication, which is necessary for maintaining transparency. Information about clients, last contacts, etc.

"S"

Situational interviews

Job interviews in which candidates are asked to describe what they would do in specific hypothetical situations.

Structured interview 1

An interview that follows a detailed list of questions prepared in advance.

Situational interviews 2

Job interviews in which candidates are asked to describe what they would do in specific hypothetical situations.

Specific forms of communication

Specific forms of communication are e.g.: result communication, risk communication, crisis communication, labor market communication, financial communication.

Stakeholders

Stakeholders are those people or organisations which are vital to the success or failure of an organization or project to reach its goals.

The primary stakeholders are:

(*a*) those needed for permission, approval and financial support

(*b*) those who are directly affected by the activities of the organization or project.
Secondary stakeholders are those who are indirectly affected.

Survey

Surveys are an important tool of communication managers. They can be aimed at researching the market, the degree of client satisfaction or a specific target group one intends to communicate with. Tools are trend panels, focus groups, personal interviews, questionnaires, etc.

"T"

Target groups

A target group is a group of people which you need to reach with your communication in order to realize a result (see communication objective). For communication purposes is better not to view them in terms of statistics but as people of flesh and blood. It is best to segment the target group as far as possible and identify the opinion leaders (name, address etc.) to whom face to face communication is possible. It is important to explore how the target group relates to the biodiversity issue and what would motivate them to act as desired.

Tertiary stakeholders

Tertiary stakeholders are those who are not affected or involved, but who can influence opinions either for or against.

"U"

Unstructured interview

An interview based on three or four main questions prepared in advance and other questions that build on what the interviewee says.

"V"

Verbal communication

Communication that uses words; may be either oral or written.

Letter: Short document using block or modified block format that goes to readers outside your organization.

Visual communication

Visual communication as the name suggests is communication through visual aid. It is the conveyance of ideas and information in forms that can be read or looked upon.

References

1. Herta A. Murphy, Herbert W. Hildebrandt, Jana P. Thomas, Irwin, *Effective Business Communication*, Mc. Graw Hill.
2. Asha Kaul, *Effective Business Communication*, Prentice Hall of India.
3. Parag Diwan, *Business Communication*, Excel Books.
4. Urmila Rai and S.M. Rai, *Business Communication*, Himalaya Publishing House.
5. P.D. Chaturvedi, Mukesh Chaturvedi, *Business Communication, Concepts, Cases and Applications*, Pearson Education.
6. K.K. Sinha, *Business Communication*, Galgotia Publishing Company.
7. Lesikar and Pettit, *Business Communication, Theory and Practice*, A.I.T.B.S., Publishers and Distributors.
8. Asha Kaul, *Business Communication*, Prentice Hall of India.
9. Website www. glasbergen. com.
10. Website www. Cartoon Stock. com.

Index

A

B

C